The **TAO** of Sobriety

Thomas Dunne Books
St. Martin's Press
New York

The
TAO
of
Sobriety

Helping You to Recover from Alcohol and Drug Addiction

David Gregson

and

Jay S. Efran, Ph.D.

Foreword by G. Alan Marlatt, Ph.D.

THOMAS DUNNE BOOKS.
An imprint of St. Martin's Press.

THE TAO OF SOBRIETY: HELPING YOU TO RECOVER FROM
ALCOHOL AND DRUG ADDICTION. Copyright © 2002 by David
Gregson and Jay S. Efran, Ph. D. Foreword copyright © 2002 by G.
Alan Marlatt, Ph. D. All rights reserved. Printed in the United States
of America. For information, address St. Martin's Press, 175 Fifth
Avenue, New York, N.Y. 10010.

www.stmartins.com

Design by Susan Walsh

ISBN 0-312-24250-6

David

To my wonderful Yiddish mother, fabulous wife,
great sons, wise and generous colleagues, and the
courageous people I serve.

Jay

This book is dedicated to the memory of
Kerry P. Heffner, who inspired students, colleagues,
clients, and friends to expand their understanding of
addictions.

Contents

Contents

Contents

Acknowledgments

The authors thank Elsa R. Efran, who shifted commas and other punctuation marks into appropriate places and saw to it that sentences were clear and complete. She helped reorganize sections of prose, instilling order and eliminating redundancy. She made sure that peculiar mixtures of pronouns or tenses would not stop the reader cold in his or her tracks. Moreover, she accomplished all of this without complaint, fostering an atmosphere of calm and quiet efficiency.

The **TAO** of Sobriety

Foreword

As a graduate student in clinical psychology in the mid-1960s, I first learned about Taoism from reading *The Way of Zen* by Alan Watts. He defined Tao as "the watercourse way," referring to the natural course that water takes as it flows effortlessly down the mountain stream into the lowland river as gravity gently guides it into the ocean. The water finds its own way, from meandering creek to thundering waterfall. Water discovers its own pace and moves easily downstream when unobstructed by outside forces (e.g., the construction of a dam that blocks its flow). The spirit of Taoism is represented by the phrase: "Don't push the river!" Or, as the old Zen saying goes, "Whatever you resist, persists."

Addiction blocks the natural flow of the "watercourse way." Central to the nature of addiction is the concept of control. Individuals who use alcohol or other drugs to control their feelings often succumb to the "illusion of control"—that they now have the power either to avoid the "low" of unpleasant experiences or to create a permanent "high" to mask the boredom of everyday life events. The more the addict seeks control by relying on alcohol or drugs as "the way," the more he or she appears to outside observers to be "hooked" and to suffer from "loss of control," considered by many experts to be the hallmark symptom of physical dependency.

From the perspective of Taoism, addiction can be equated on a psychological level with the inability to accept the fullness of the present moment. For the addict, acceptance of the "Here and Now" is replaced by a future focus on the "Next Fix." The urges and craving for substances that promise to ease the suffering or transform boredom into a positive high are a constant distraction. Meditation provides an antidote for medication and the ongoing focus on the Next Fix. As stated by one experienced meditation teacher in response to his student's concern about the future: "Nothing happens next. This is it!"

The noted analyst Carl Jung once referred to alcoholics and addicts as "frustrated mystics." Jung believed that many people who are attracted to alcohol and drugs are drawn to the experience of "altered states" because of their ostensible similarity to transcendental spiritual experiences. His interest in the link between seeking spiritual enlightenment and seeking solace from the spirits in the bottle proved to be influential in the founding of Alcoholics Anonymous and the ubiquitous Twelve-Step model of recovery.

For those "frustrated mystics" who reject the Christian orientation and the emphasis on salvation through allegiance to a "Higher Power," Taoism and Buddhism provide an alternative pathway leading to personal awakening and spiritual enlightenment. Buddhists speak of the Eight-

Fold Path as an alternative to the Twelve Steps—both may provide optional routes to the same overall destination.

Unlike the disease model, which defines addiction solely in biological or physiological terms (e.g., addiction as a disease of the brain or alcoholism as a genetic disorder), Eastern spiritual approaches are more likely to describe addiction as a "disease of the mind." To define addiction as a disease is to adopt a dichotomous stance— someone either has the disease or does not have it. In contrast, Taoism and Buddhism share the assumption that addictive problems can be placed on a continuum ranging from minor to major problems. This position is congruent with the definition of Taoism as the Middle Way, a position of balance between the extremes of self-indulgence (addiction) and absolute self-denial. As one of my clients who found a new position of balance through her own meditation experiences recently stated, "Through my meditation practice, I have discovered that I no longer have to be dictated to by my thoughts about needing to drink whenever things are not going the way I want them to—I now can accept my urges and craving without giving into them automatically the way I used to." It is interesting to note in this regard that the Latin root of the word addiction ("addicere," to give assent) is the same as for the terms "dictator" and "dictation." Taoism and meditation practice provide the pathway to freedom from the dictator thoughts of the addicted mind. As stated by the authors, "Instead of excluding, denying, or resisting ugly or problematic aspects of life, the Taoist suggests that such elements be 'allowed to be' in a way that nourishes rather than destroys our enjoyment of living."

There is much for readers to like in this fine book by Gregson and Efran. The material presented provides a roadmap for a Journey of Discovery that goes far beyond the more traditional "Recovery" model of addiction treatment. Those who are willing to travel on the Taoist pathway will find numerous exercises and other "homework" assignments provided by the authors to facilitate the process of self-discovery. To take but one example, the authors describe a unique and effective means of dealing with the conflicting voices and mental directives associated with the "inner dialogue" that occurs in the minds of many people with addiction problems. Here the reader is urged to foster and support the role of a psychological "manager" capable of negotiating the conflicting demands (e.g., urges and cravings for substance use). The role of the "manager" is to foster acceptance and detachment from the thoughts and feelings that otherwise promote the continuation of the addictive behavior. Completion of the exercises presented in the book will help readers "lighten up" in their otherwise self-critical and self-defeating thoughts and feelings—the guilt, shame, and self-criticism associated with the stigma of addiction. Much of this material is brought to life by the inclusion of clinical case studies that illustrate the general principles. The authors, both experienced therapists in the addictions field, also offer some personal examples to add additional interest.

I recommend this book highly for readers who are searching for an alternative path in their quest to escape the psychological confines of addiction. All it takes is your interest and time to take the first step in exploring this new and exciting pathway of discovery. As the old saying goes, "Where there's a will, there's a way." For readers who bring their own sense of motivation—the Will to change—Taoism provides the Way. All in all, it's quite a trip!

G. Alan Marlatt, Ph.D.
Professor of Psychology
Director, Addictive Behaviors Research Center
University of Washington

CHAPTER 1

Introduction

This workbook is intended for those of you who want help with serious drug or alcohol problems. It can equip you with tools powerful enough to cut through the chains that bind you to these chemical tyrants. It will train you to use psychological know-how to dissolve the barriers that separate you from health and personal satisfaction. Using the concepts we provide, you can make a huge difference in your life.

The truth of the matter is that, as a human being, *you have always had the capacity to create a future different from what past events predict.* This is what makes members of our species so unique. In this book, we propose ways to get in touch with that continuously available creative capacity, enabling you to turn your life around at will. Our goal is that you will discover how to live more powerfully, compassionately, and creatively—without, of course, having to depend on alcohol or drugs. All we require of you is that you read the material, keep an open mind, and do the exercises we call "discoveries." These are engineered to facilitate deeper understanding so that you can move from knowing to doing, from *right under-standings* to *right actions*.

In short, when the storm is blowing furiously and you are lost and desperately in need of directions to get you home, we intend—through the medium of this book—to be there to show the way.

A Word About Twelve-Step Programs

Many people reading this book probably belong to Twelve-Step fellowships. Those groups regularly make a profound difference in people's lives. Alcoholics Anonymous or AA, the model for all other Twelve-Step groups, has pioneered efforts to restore humanity to those who are locked into patterns of chemical dependency. Our intention is to assist those working Twelve-Step programs as well as those who may not choose to join a Twelve-Step group.

What Is the Tao?

For thousands of years, Eastern traditions like Taoism, Buddhism, and Zen have helped individuals find inner peace. The wisdom contained in these disciplines is a useful antidote to the selfishness and egoism that characterize so much of Western culture. Americans and other Westerners are preoccupied with self-sufficiency and independence, partly in the belief that such attitudes lead directly to the promised land of happiness and satisfaction. In fact, too much focus on oneself usually does just the opposite—leaving people confused about their goals and alienated from each other. Albert Einstein warned that "the illusion that we are separate from one another is an optical delusion of our consciousness." He realized that the conventional Western recipe for success, emphasizing individual achievement and competition, is often a formula for loneliness, isolation, and despair. The Eastern views we will be talking about advise a more holistic, compassionate, and relational perspective.

Don't worry—the point of this book is not to turn anyone into an Eastern mystic. For centuries, traditions such as Taoism and Buddhism have provided practical guidance to flesh-and-blood individuals seeking peace, well-being, and harmony against the background of the real world's hustle and bustle. Clients with whom we have worked have regularly found these perspectives useful. They provide realistic, no-nonsense solutions to everyday problems. On the one hand, our message is profoundly spiritual—it envisions a universe in which we all belong and have worth. At the same time, it is eminently down-to-earth, describing a method for obtaining relief from the pain that motivates alcohol and drug abuse.

The vision we are proposing is sometimes called "seeing with a third eye." It is about noticing the big picture that is ordinarily outside our awareness, and then using the resulting insights to enhance our everyday existence. It is about performing a balancing act that successfully juggles opposites that Westerners often consider irreconcilable. For instance, many people feel torn between their religious commitments and their material ambitions. They pray at church and make money at the office but find it difficult to mesh these apparently divergent activities. To us, however, all activities are both spiritual and material. We are not using the term "spiritual" to refer to formal religious practices or some rarefied set of ethereal goals. Instead, we are referring to a sweet serenity that can pervade all aspects of life—an image of perfection, completion, and connection that can be just as applicable to business transactions as religious rituals. Moreover, the spirituality we have in mind is as pertinent to the atheist as the religious zealot.

The material/spiritual duality is an example of a pair of terms that define one another, the way *up* defines *down*. Similarly, concepts such as completion, transcendence, and peace are meaningful only in relation to their opposite—the fragmented, competitive rat race of daily existence. In Eastern philosophy, the dance of opposites is acknowledged and accepted as the essence of the game of life. The trick is to learn to float effortlessly in the space such divergent poles create. For example, the Eastern sage grasps (and enjoys) the "joke" of life without ignoring or denigrating people's suffering. From an Eastern perspective, life is inevitably tragicomic—neither entirely gloomy nor simply a barrel of laughs.

The term *Tao* means "the way." It provides a kind of road map for living. The Eastern philosophies from which we borrow converge to define a unique middle path that seems to help people navigate the complexities of experience. Paradoxically, both virtue and sin are understood from within an overarching framework of unconditional love, acceptance, and compassion. Instead of excluding, denying, or resisting ugly or problematic aspects of life, the Taoist suggests that such elements be "allowed to be" in a way that nourishes rather than destroys our enjoyment of living. This was the theme of a cartoon we recently saw. It portrayed a Zen elevator that, in addition to the usual up and down options, provided a special Zen button marked CONTENT RIGHT WHERE YOU ARE. Of course, some people confuse contentment with passivity and resignation. They think that the message of Zen is to leave things the way they are—to make do with the status quo. In later chapters we will address this common misconception.

The world has changed dramatically since Taoism and related Eastern traditions began. So, we will be translating the insights of these teachings into modern lingo. We presume that the ancient sages, including Lao Tzu, the sixth-century (B.C.) founder of Taoism, and the Buddha, who lived and taught twenty-five hundred years ago, could and would do the same if they were alive today. After all, these men of wisdom warned against anyone becoming too attached to particular forms of rhetoric or ritual—including their own.

For some people, mood-altering chemicals have served as shortcuts to Nirvana. Undoubtedly, drugs can provide profound (albeit fleeting) experiences of being whole, complete, and self-satisfied. The path we follow in *The Tao of Sobriety* creates that same light-hearted experience of wholeness and relationship, but without the physical, psychological, and social detriments chemical routes entail. In the next chapter, you will see an example of how one individual maintained his sobriety by practicing innocence in spirit, a principle we will describe later. Throughout the book, we will present additional concrete examples of how these time-tested ideas, which may at first seem abstract, can be put to work to help you achieve your goals.

CHAPTER 2

Alcohol, Drugs, and You

People do not wake up one morning on the sunny side of life and suddenly decide to throw everything away and mess up their lives with drugs and alcohol. The world just doesn't work that way. People always do what they do for good and sufficient reasons. So, regardless of your past circumstances, actions, and feelings, we intend to think of you as *innocent in spirit*.

In our experience, individuals who believe, deep down, that they are fundamentally flawed are much more likely to behave ineffectively and irresponsibly. On the other hand, people who are in touch with their own essential innocence are better equipped to handle life appropriately and efficiently. Thus, we are about to suggest a simple exercise—the first of many in this book—designed to help you determine whether you are indeed innocent in spirit, as we maintain, or whether you are unworthy of your own support and admiration. So, follow the instructions and take the next few moments to examine where you stand on the fundamental issue of guilt, particularly in the realm of substance use.

DISCOVERY 1: Innocence in Spirit

Do the Following:

Recall whether you ever woke up one morning feeling truly happy and at peace with the world, and then decided something like "Today is a perfect day to mess up my life with drugs or alcohol!" Now that you have taken time to think about it seriously, did you ever *truly* make that kind of decision? If you did, perhaps you are guilty after all. Otherwise, it seems to us that you are innocent of willfully and purposely screwing things up.

~

What did you come up with, guilty or innocent? If you did not knowingly make choices that were calculated to ruin your life, there are no rational grounds for considering yourself blameworthy in connection with substance misuse. Who would intentionally go out of their way and freely choose the hell of chemical addiction? If you have feelings of guilt and indulge in bouts of self-condemnation, these are based on an incomplete or faulty analysis of life's causes and effects. Moreover, as we shall demonstrate later, these guilt trips contribute nothing to your well-being or the rehabilitation of your zest for living.

Aaron's Story

Aaron was a man of about forty-five. He was a member of AA and had been sober for approximately ten years.

He sought counseling from one of the authors because he feared that the emotional roller coaster he was on would precipitate a relapse. He had recently been told that his twenty-one-year-old son had a drinking problem that paralleled his own. The son, who was living with his mother—Aaron's ex-wife—had cut off communication with him years before. The boy resented the heavy toll his father's drinking (and the acrimonious divorce and custody battle that followed) had taken on the family.

Aaron was a faithful AA member, doing the Twelve Steps, participating in his home group with a dedication others admired, and becoming a sponsor to many new members. However, he could not break through his own self-anger and guilt. He confided that despite his allegiance to the AA program, he did not really believe that alcoholism was a disease. This left him feeling a bit estranged even though he continued to "work his program."

In Aaron's first counseling session, the author told him that whether or not he had a disease was beside the point. Unless he could prove that he had freely chosen to become a drunk and alienate his family, he would have to be considered "innocent of all charges." Aaron began to laugh out loud. He realized, of course, that it is ludicrous to think that anybody would freely choose to mess up his or her life so completely. After the laughter came tears, and the upset that had been festering for so long just evaporated.

In the next session, Aaron began sorting out the complex feelings he had toward his own father. His father had been a jazz musician who, like many hipsters in the '40s and '50s, had been hooked on drugs and alcohol. Growing up, Aaron did not get to see much of his dad, who traveled extensively with the band. When his father was at home he could be a miserable tyrant. On the other hand, when he got high, he was a great guy—singing, playing his instrument, and telling stories. Aaron both idolized and hated his father. Ironically, he blamed him for many of the same failings for which his own son was now blaming him.

A session later (this case progressed with unusual rapidity), Aaron managed to get his son to come in. The boy was clearly furious and had much to get off his chest. However, after they had discussed details of the family pattern of alcohol abuse—going back several generations— the son agreed to attend an AA meeting. Aaron's need for individual counseling diminished and, six months later, he called to report that both he and his son were still doing well.

We mention this case because it illustrates the value of reassessing your essential innocence. There is an old saying that most people have to be dragged screaming into paradise. Therefore, although we have just presented a beginning logic for considering oneself innocent in the realm of substance misuse, many—perhaps most—readers will be entertaining a series of "yes, buts" rather than agreeing to walk down the lighter path of innocence we are depicting. If you fall into that category, you will probably take some convincing to believe that it is all right, even *healthy*, for you to embrace your innocence of spirit. We are confident that we have rationality and logic on our side, and in succeeding chapters we will attempt to prove it. However, even when faced with facts and logic, people often refuse to give up their own dreadful self-appraisals. They somehow feel psychologically naked without their familiar—negative—beliefs. So, one aim of this book is to drag you into paradise, or more accurately, to provide the navigation tools to enable you to amble over in that direction under your own steam, and at your own pace.

Reality-Altering Substances

Alcohol and drugs change or mitigate your experience of reality. If you feel one way before taking a mind-altering substance, you can be sure you will feel differently afterward. Otherwise, what would be the point? Note that we are using the phrase "feel differently" to cover a multitude of shifts in thinking, feeling, perceiving, and behaving— the whole ball of wax.

Drugs and alcohol take you up, down, and sideways. They put you somewhere other than where you started out, and they do this magnificently. Perhaps that is why mood-altering substances have had such a long history. As you may know, there is evidence of beer brewing over five thousand years ago. In fact, an adventuresome brewing company recently formulated a modern beer based on a chemical analysis of ancient Egyptian dregs. Furthermore, whenever psychoactive substances have been popular, there have been sanctions and prohibitions against their use. Those rules and regulations attest both to the human craving for altering subjective experience and to the havoc such indulgences often create.

As most of us know, drugs—what we might call "reality mitigants"—are generally habit-forming, both pharmacologically and psychologically. In the jargon of the field, they create "dependencies." The word *depend* comes from the Latin *dependere,* literally meaning "to hang down from." Now, that's an interesting image: You hanging down like a leaf, more or less helpless, flapping in the wind in connection with some chemical substance.

Another way to say this is that chemical dependency is a temporary solution to an immediate problem. Unfortunately, the solution usually creates new and additional troubles that are worse than the original difficulty. In other words, chemical solutions work, but the costs are high. It's like running from a bully in a schoolyard. The more we run, the bigger the bully seems and the smaller we feel. Furthermore, the more we run, the more we establish a pattern of running. Once set up, this ego-belittling cycle of avoiding or hiding becomes a way of life. Although the opposite strategy—facing the bully—is frightening and difficult, the potential rewards are immense. When we stand up to bullies, we expand our world, gaining the freedom to venture into the territories the bullies previously dominated. Moreover, because bullies are larger in fantasy than reality, confrontations with them are usually less painful than we had imagined. Running adds heft to our opponents, standing pat helps cut them down to size. The really good news is that it is never too late in life to face the fears that we have allowed to bully us.

More good news is that you do not have to face your problems alone. This book, for instance, is here to coach you. In addition, many of you have counselors, family members, friends, and organizations to cheer you on in fighting the good fight.

Consider for a moment the virtues of gaining mastery

over your fears and repossessing all of your experience! As you become empowered to stand firmly, lovingly, and creatively at your own center, psychoactive substances *have* to become increasingly irrelevant. By figuring out how to be responsible for your experience, especially the scary and ugly portions, you reposition yourself as ruler of your own kingdom, rather than the slavish victim of unwanted interlopers.

More Gain Than Pain

We are not suggesting that reclaiming your rightful personal territory is a breeze. You ingest mood-mitigating chemicals to avoid painful and seemingly uncontrollable aspects of life. Therefore, the distress these mitigants have held at bay can be expected to pay a return visit when you threaten to abandon your allegiance to these substances. Instead of feeling great and liberated when you give up drugs, you may initially be faced with a flood of confusing and disturbing reactions. And we are not even talking about the physical discomforts connected with the body's need to adjust its biochemistry.

Think of it this way: In a conditioning or bodybuilding program, a burning sensation can be a welcome sign of progress. Similarly, each piece of distress you experience as you move back into a drug-free reality is a validation that you have reversed engines—you are no longer running. As with all other daring missions, you can count on some agonizing moments of uncertainty. At times, the entire project will seem like folly. The transitional torments may not seem worth it. However, doubts and obstacles will disappear as you demonstrate to yourself that you are determined to move forward.

Looking back, you are apt to wonder why your misgivings loomed so large. Like a school bully who has been confronted, your fear goblins will have diminished in size. We are convinced that completing the "mission possible" set out in this book will tip the scales in favor of living contentedly, in a way that automatically reduces your need to misuse chemicals.

Beyond Alcohol and Drugs

The strategy detailed in this workbook entails *lightening up* about everything: drugs, personal problems, life itself. Please avoid the paradoxical pitfall of becoming too grim and serious about lightening up. Attempting to reach the enlightenment of a chemical-free existence through endless effort and struggle is, at the very least, doing it the hard way.

Some people successfully give up drugs without becoming particularly enlightened. They end up sober but somber! From our perspective they have only handled half the problem. The goal of the scheme we propose is to create positive effects that spread, creating satisfaction and appropriateness in all areas of life: self, family, physical health, finances, work, play, and community. Denying or avoiding pain and discomfort is not the same as gaining mastery over it or becoming light about life. Denial and avoidance can be side effects of drug use; enlightenment is at the opposite end of the spectrum.

To repeat: The goal of this workbook is to assist you

in giving up addictive substances and to help you discover that the bullies you have been avoiding or struggling with are actually cowards in disguise. You have the power to defeat them! One of the authors, David, had a serious drug addiction. Using the wisdom offered here, he was able to overcome his problem and go on to a richly satisfying and productive life. Drugs are no longer an issue for him and will never be again! At root, he is very much like you.

In the next chapter, we begin our quest for a more fulfilling future. It begins with a simple explanation of how our minds work, and why cerebral functions so often get in our way rather than helping us achieve our dreams.

CHAPTER 3

I Think, Therefore I Am

What we routinely call "mind" or "consciousness," the heart of our soulful being, is dependent on our ability to think and use language. Without words and symbols, we are not fully human.

As human beings, we not only think, but we think *about* our own thinking. This reflective ability is what separates us from most other species and from even the cleverest of machines. Many animal species engage in simple forms of information processing. However, few of them are blessed (and cursed) with the possibility of self-awareness—that is, with thinking about who is doing the thinking. It is doubtful, for example, that bears or wolves wonder about their purpose in the universe, or, for that matter, whether it was a stroke of good or bad fortune to have been born a bear or a wolf. They do not ask themselves the sorts of questions human beings ponder endlessly, such as "Who am I?" "Am I a winner or a loser?" and so on. Bears and wolves exist, but they are incapable of being inquisitive about their own existence.

Our human capacity for reflective thinking makes possible most of the achievements of which we are proudest, but at the same time it also perpetuates the heaviness with which many of us troop through life. Cats and dogs do not worry about where the next meal will come from or whether they are as cute and winsome as the kitten or puppy next door. However, humans evaluate virtually everything in rock-hard, personal terms. They worry about yesterday and they worry about tomorrow. No wonder the use of mood-altering substances is so universal! Our reflective minds spin elaborate webs of judgments and comparisons that both enthrall and entrap. They give us something to strive for, but they also fuel endless doubts and regrets.

Odd Insights About Us

Something that is particularly odd about thinking is that it forces us to act as if we were two or more different people living in the same body. In other words, one of "us" almost continually observes and talks about what the other one of us is doing.

For example, while you are taking a morning shower, a voice in your head may suddenly announce that it is time to turn off the water and get dressed for work. At the same time, another "you" is apt to object, arguing that there is still plenty of time to bask under the warm flow of water. "What's the big rush?" that second voice asks. In the ensuing discussion, it isn't quite clear who is arguing with whom. Which "you" is opting for getting dressed, and who is he or she trying to convince? Moreover, is there anyone *in there* who can referee this debate or determine which voice is winning? Among these contentious internal voices, which should be considered the real you? Sometimes the whole process seems like the mental equivalent of a tug-of-war between the right and left hands of the same person. The harder one hand pulls, the harder the other resists. It is a wonder anything gets done! And yet it does.

These internal conversations seem like debates between at least two participants arguing opposite positions. Sometimes, however, a commentator also seems to be present— a kind of shadowy background character who hovers on the sidelines, waiting to see which of the two major players is gaining the upper hand. In various forms, such self-conversations go on virtually all day long as a background accompaniment to our other activities. These internal dialogues can be calming and self-congratulatory, or they can be nagging and assaultive. The inner voices alternately gloat, rejoice, scold, and condemn. In talking to ourselves, we may even find ourselves making pronouncements that take us by surprise. Imagine—the capacity to be scandalized by our own inner thoughts! During internal exchanges, other "selves" beyond those first two speakers may show up, all insisting on having their say. It can get very noisy inside.

Who's the Boss?

The self-reflective conversations we are describing shape who we believe ourselves to be. Moreover, in these discussions, we are easily swayed by our own opinions. We pay attention to our internal dialogue even though the points of view expressed are often based on flimsy evidence and frequently defy the ordinary rules of logic and consistency. Even brilliant individuals with well-earned reputations for clear thinking can be naively susceptible to the beliefs their own inner voices express. They may have developed effective tools for questioning and evaluating the judgments of others, but they are pushovers when it comes to critically assessing their own beliefs.

Our own internal opinions fluctuate wildly from one moment to the next. One minute we convince ourselves that we are the kindest, smartest, and sanest people on the entire planet; the next minute we decide that we are immature, idiotic, and selfish. Such self-appraisals go from altruistic and rational to malevolent and crazy in the time it takes a few neurons to fire.

In debates with outside authority, the internal voices have the edge. For example, as you are reading this workbook, you will undoubtedly be checking with your inner voices to see if the ideas we are presenting mesh with what you already believe. Are these guys on the money or are they out in left field somewhere? A thumbs-down from those inner voices can mean that the rest of what we have written is history, at least as far as the dialogue between us and you is concerned. As writers, we have to hope that your inner voices will remain open to our message rather than prematurely dismissing what we have to say.

In other words, inner dialogue is the ultimate judge of what a person accepts as true. External opinions are tested against internal convictions. Conclusions reached through interior dialogue stick unless they are revoked by the person's own subsequent thinking. So when people are overly self-critical and reject potentially sound advice—such as the kind we hope to be offering in this book—they are suffering as much at their own hands as at the hands of others.

Incredibly, people have no direct control over how these crucial inner discussions unfold. As we will explain in detail later, it is as if people are simply the physical space or location where such conversations take place. As the conversation develops, they are privy to what is being said "in there," but they cannot necessarily predict or determine the outcome. They do not know for sure when they will leave the shower and go and get dressed until they notice themselves reaching for the knobs to turn off the water.

Given the utter importance of this internal thinking process, it is surprising that we are not taught more about it in school. We are often told *what* to think, but not how thoughts happen or how they affect our life patterns. One purpose of this book is to assist you in developing a more sophisticated and useful understanding of your own mental operating system.

Journeying Deeper into Being

As we have said, who you consider "you" to be is tied to the nature of the conversations you have with yourself. Notice, for example, that it is difficult for you to get out of bed while having thoughts like "I'm just too weary to get up." Phrases like "just too weary" are incompatible with springing into action.

If you know anything about hypnosis, or have seen it demonstrated, you may realize that the process of self-conversation is the central mechanism of hypnotic suggestion. Good hypnotic subjects reproduce the hypnotist's instructions in their own self-dialogue. For instance, when the hypnotist tells them that their left arm is too heavy to lift, they immediately repeat that instruction to themselves, often adding embellishments that help transform the idea into a believable reality. As they think in harmony with the suggestion, their arm almost magically becomes difficult to lift. It begins to feel heavy as lead, just as the hypnotist implied that it would. It seems increasingly stuck in its current position. The self-talk of good hypnotic subjects colors their perceptions, progressively enhancing the power of the hypnotist's suggestions.

In contrast, poor hypnotic subjects engage in a kind of conversational mutiny. Their internal dialogue veers off in all sorts of unpredictable directions. They may tell themselves that the suggestion isn't working, that it is impossible for a physically healthy arm to suddenly become too heavy to lift, and that they are probably not really hypnotized. These thoughts works against experiencing the effect the hypnotist is suggesting.

Try the following simple experiment. Think about your tongue. It sits in your mouth all day. It has nowhere else to go. It is never able to go off duty. It cannot relax and lie still, because it is in constant danger of getting caught between your teeth on one side or another. In fact, your tongue seems just a bit too large to be able to rest comfortably in its allotted space. Therefore, it is almost continually darting about, shifting this way and that to avoid getting bitten.

By planting these thoughts about your tongue, we have tried to steer your self-conversation in particular directions. Before you read the previous paragraph, you paid no attention to your tongue. It was a non-issue. However, by focusing on it, we hopefully made something normally unobtrusive become increasingly problematic. The point is that whenever your conversation with yourself changes—and the reason for the change may not matter—you become a somewhat different individual, with different priorities, problems, and preoccupations.

The words we use with ourselves can have magical properties. Although saying you can fly (without airline tickets) won't make it so, many of our everyday limitations are self-imposed, deriving from the position we take in our internal dialogue. Thoughts that show up inside our heads influence our attitudes and shape our actions. Of course, it also works the other way around. How we behave and what we perceive affect the content of our daytime fantasies and nighttime dreams.

A Practical Example

Recently, a colleague complained that he was unable to quit smoking. To every suggestion people made, he said, "That won't work!" or "I already tried that." Soon he succeeded in discouraging people from trying to help, reinforcing his own bleak assessment that his situation was hopeless. His plan to quit smoking was partially handicapped by his self-conversation, which automatically defined all of his efforts as futile. As Ralph Waldo Emerson wrote, "As long as a man stands in his own way, everything seems to be in his way."

DISCOVERY 2: Listening to the Internal Conversation

To solidify the ideas we have been discussing, first reflect for a minute or two on the following statement: "My mind is filled with conversations I am having with myself." To do this, you will probably have to repeat the statement to yourself a couple of times. Now also reflect on the fact that the aspect of you who just spoke that sentence was talking to some other part of you, who heard and understood what was being said. In other words, there was a speaker and a listener. If you like, you can repeat the sentence to yourself several more times to see if this is indeed true of your experience. Is there any way to get around the fact that there is a speaker and a listener in there? Of course, it is easier to notice the speaker than the listener; the listener isn't saying anything. However, someone has to be listening. Otherwise, what would be the point of holding a conversation with yourself?

Next, silently repeat this simple question to yourself: "What time is it?" Repeat this several times. We want you to take notice of the fact that when you think, some part of you speaks and another part of you listens to what is spoken.

~

Who Are You?

Within that dynamic duo, the listener and speaker, who are you? Are you the one speaking, the one being addressed, or a bystander eavesdropping on the conversation? In fact, the mystery gets deeper: When there are internal debates—which is much of the time—whose side are "you" on? In our earlier example, were you the one voting for getting out of the shower right away or the one stalling for more time? Perhaps you were that neutral figure listening to the other two voices argue.

Trying to sort out this stuff can be headache-producing. When people dwell on the details of their internal dialogue and attempt to figure out who is who, it is as if they are standing between two mirrors, watching their image bounce back and forth. So, let's simplify matters. We propose that humans are describable—drumroll please—as *a space where thoughts show up*. In other words, you are neither the speaker, the listener, nor the neutral observer, but the location in which the entire conversation happens. It is as if you are a theater in which various internal plays are produced and presented. In that theater of the mind, many opportunities and possibilities exist.

DISCOVERY 3: The Space That Is You

Take some time now to thoroughly reflect on this idea: Who we are as human beings is a space—a psychological theater—where thoughts and inner conversations show up. We are not simply the contents of any particular show or story line, but the place where all of our stories play themselves out. Different plots come and go, but the theater itself remains a constant.

Note that when you are aware that you are the playhouse and not just the play, it helps you detach from any particular disempowering drama that happens to be showing at a particular point in time. At any point, there is the possibility of a different script being delivered by the production department, perhaps turning a depressing or uninteresting presentation into a riveting attraction.

~

The One and the Other

To reiterate, as humans, it is helpful to think of ourselves as the space in which internal dialogues show up. Some of these conversations are about health, satisfaction, and general well-being. Others are far less cheery. Perhaps the worst are the highly repetitive, predictable, joyless scripts that get performed over and over. And, of course, it is when one of these familiar tragedies is on the bill that we are most apt to duck out into the lobby for a fortifying drink or two.

Ordinarily, we humans picture ourselves as being a single entity, a "self" seated at the controls of some sort of elaborate cerebral switchboard. In fact, our ability to converse with ourselves means that there are a minimum of two folks up there. There has to be sort of a split. No split, no conversation. No conversation, no us. It's that simple. If you say to yourself "I think I ought to call home," there has to be someone making that proposal and someone else deciding whether or not to act on it.

Higher Math: The One and the Many

But we are usually more than just two selves. When we wake up in the morning, we do not have quite the same conversation with ourselves that we might have after our first cup of coffee. When we are embroiled in a marital disagreement, we are not thinking and feeling the same way we might be when holding and comforting a small child. When we are out carousing with the gang we are different than when we are visiting an elderly aunt. If our children were to catch us in the middle of a lovemaking session, would they recognize us as the parents with whom they are familiar? Is the person who gets drunk or high the same self that promised to remain abstinent?

For that matter, are we the same person now that we were as a child? Haven't we changed a good deal over just the past decade? In fact, so much about us changes from moment to moment and year to year that it is almost nonsensical to consider ourselves the same human being from one year to the next. Yet, there is indeed a similarity to the space we identify as ourselves. The theater stays the same even though the show keeps changing. The content shifts, but the location continues to seem familiar. Moreover, that space is large enough and flexible enough to house an entire menagerie of characters, personalities, viewpoints, and performances. Therefore, we might say that we are "the one and the many," a single space that hosts a veritable cacophony of competing mental voices.

DISCOVERY 4: Discovering Who You Are

Take some time now and reflect upon the fact that
who you are is the one and the many—not just a
single self, but a performance space in which a
hodgepodge of thoughts and opinions show up.
Most likely you have grown up with the image
of a single miniature person—sometimes called a
homunculus—sitting at the controls. However, it
would be more accurate to picture a bunch of
squabbling busybodies up there, each trying to
make themselves heard above the general din.

~

Who's Got the Power?

If we think of the mind as a kind of unruly executive
committee, it might be useful to provide some reliable
leadership. Particularly if the existing power brokers have
been recommending substance use as the major method
for dealing with life's pain and confusion, it may be time
to throw out the old regime and vote a new party into
office.

To begin the process of strengthening the leadership,
reflect on who, among those perennially rowdy committee members, is best suited to preside over the rest of
the quarrelsome gang. The goal is to identify a conversational voice that can move the group toward a more
satisfying life strategy. Then, we will provide techniques
for empowering that voice, making it more confident and
reliable.

Among your many competing internal voices, who is capable of leading you toward a healthy and satisfying future—without the need for high-cost mood-mitigating substances? Who can come forward from among the many and represent the best in you? Is there someone in there willing to do what it takes to free you from the need to dilute your experience of reality with chemicals?

It is not only likely that there is such an inner representative, it is also likely that we are communicating with that aspect of you *right now*. At other times, negative voices will undoubtedly grab the microphone. However, if you are continuing to read this, something is keeping you engaged in a conversation about living a life devoid of alcohol and drug dependency. We want you to begin to notice, isolate, distinguish, and thereby *strengthen* this leadership aspect of your inner dialogue.

The idea is to have a conversation emerge that can guide you through the rest of this book and on to a life of well-being. This leader doesn't have to start off all-powerful. Even tiny embers, if fanned efficiently, can grow to be powerful flames. Leaders develop strength and wisdom if they have a clear mandate and are well-coached. We are here to help with the coaching.

The leader we want to contact and empower is undoubtedly already there in your mind, albeit in a weakened position relative to other committee members. From now on, we will be addressing this potential commander-in-chief as "the manager." As the book progresses, we will be directing some comments specifically to the attention of this executive officer. In fact, we do exactly that in the next two paragraphs.

As manager, you may still be a little confused about

your executive ability and potential. The trick is to stay focused on basics—*to be the one who represents a commitment to well-being and the expression of love and compassion for yourself and for others.* Having a mighty purpose is empowering, and there is hardly a larger or bolder purpose than taking a stand for well-being and love. If, at this early stage, such a bold commitment does not feel real, we suggest that you simply try it on for size. Who knows, by the end of this book it just might fit.

Whenever things seem adrift, you—as manager—can always draw strength by reminding yourself of this basic commitment to well-being and love. As your power and influence increase, that commitment will become increasingly real, and the need to use drugs and alcohol will automatically dissipate. This is our prediction and promise. In the next chapter, we will have more to say about your job as manager.

CHAPTER 4

Managing the Mind

As the newly emerging manager of your mind space, you need to reflect on the commitment we discussed in the previous chapter—maximizing well-being and expressing love for self and others. That is all you care about. As manager, that is all you are about. This voyage of self-discovery involves learning to hold on to the reins of power despite the distractions of various negative internal voices.

You can expect your power as manager to grow as you develop a successful track record of consistent and reliable performance. With practice, the amount of time and effort it takes to restore order after a lapse into negativity will decrease. Actually, the entire committee of internal voices secretly wants you to succeed. They want what you want—increased well-being, self-expression, and compassion for self and others. However, it will be a while before "the others" admit to appreciating your leadership. In the meantime, they cannot be expected to be cooperative.

DISCOVERY 5: Enhancing the Manager

What mental or visual image will support your role as the supreme manager of a fractious committee of internal voices? Would it be helpful to dress yourself up in presidential or prime-ministerial garb? Might you want a leaderlike title? Perhaps it is sufficient that you be addressed as "sir" or "Madame Manager"? Would it help for you to have an engraved gavel? Should there be a special fanfare whenever you are about to make an important announcement or render a policy decision? Do whatever it takes in your mind's eye to get clarity about your role as the manager of internal voices. You will be the spokesperson whose job it will be to lead the entire group of voices to success. Once you have developed a clear image of yourself as manager, you—as manager—can take a short siesta until it's time for the next exercise.

∼

Biker Stan

Stan came in for counseling one day and everybody in the office just stared. He was an ex-biker covered with body art. He had muscles to spare and plenty of attitude. When he was in his early twenties, he and a group of friends kidnapped his dad. They staged a mock trial and punished him for his abusive treatment of Stan, almost beating him to death. Stan then joined a notorious biker gang and became a feared enforcer. For years, violence and drugs had been his armor against feelings of vulnerability and fear. But Stan had a young son who was becoming increasingly rebellious. When he looked into his son's eyes, Stan could see that simply laying down the law would not make enough of a difference in his son's life. He needed to find a way to express his commitment and compassion. Although Stan had been clean and sober for about nine years, he still had trouble letting down his guard and allowing his love to show. He cared deeply for his son. He ached to be closer to him, yet it was a struggle for him to get beyond his tough-guy role long enough to communicate his feelings. At a joint session with his son, he finally managed to awkwardly blurt out the simple but eloquent message, "I love you."

∼

Think of your manager's internal drive for love and well-being as a muscle that must be isolated and exercised to gain strength. Initially, you may not even be consciously aware that such a muscle exists. Certainly trying to lift too much too soon can be futile and frustrating. However, by recognizing the muscle and working it, you will become capable of handling jobs that at first seemed hopeless.

We should mention at this time that it is not important (or possible) for a manager—any manager—to get everything right all the time. Even the most skilled executive must, on occasion, ask for help. A good support system can include a group like AA, a savvy counselor, a religious advisor, a loving partner, and understanding friends and family. Also, every leader must cultivate a genuine, ferocious commitment. Persistence will win out over even the strongest naysayers. Giving up is easy and is remarkably simple to justify. Commitment, on the other hand, remains the only true path to satisfaction. Great leaders must declare their absolute commitment to carry a job through to completion, no matter what. Here is the way President Calvin Coolidge put it:

> Nothing in the world can take the place of persistence. Talent will not; nothing is more common than unsuccessful men with talent. Genius will not; unrewarded genius is almost a proverb. Education will not; the world is full of educated derelicts. Persistence and determination alone are omnipotent.

DISCOVERY 6: Making a Commitment

Once again, we need to ask your manager to step forward and carry out this exercise. As manager, you have been identified as the internal voice representing well-being and the expression of love. Use this exercise as an opportunity to formally declare your commitment to those values. If you like, you could think of this as your formal inauguration into the managerial role. Let's make this a forceful process that helps cement a new set of priorities.

As manager, are you ready to proceed, perhaps with gavel in hand? You are about to explicitly declare your intentions. This includes acknowledging your willingness to stand up to any number of internal mental thugs who would like to derail the process. It means carving out a pathway toward greater well-being, love, and compassion even though you may not yet know exactly what those words imply or how to proceed. All you need at this juncture is an initial hunch or intuition that a stand for well-being, love, and compassion is where it's at. Up until now, it is likely that a variety of other positions and goals have dominated your mind space.

To take the stand we are proposing, you need to repeat (for the benefit of your entire internal community) a statement such as the following: "I declare that I now take a stand for maximizing love and well-being, for myself and for others." You do not need to use those specific words. Perhaps you can come up with a wording that is more personally meaningful, but using our words or your own, make a declaration of your commitment. Or, if you feel that you are not ready to make that kind of commitment, tell yourself why this is not yet the right time to do so.

~

For the moment, do not worry about sharing your managerial commitment with other people. Since you are new on the job, you might be afraid that you will not be able to keep your word and you would then feel worse for having prematurely publicized a bogus stand. Good leaders do not necessarily rush into things. So, if you are reluctant at this time to share your commitment with friends and relatives, that is okay. Similarly, if you were unable to declare the commitment to yourself, don't worry about it. If you continue on with this book, you are in effect *being* the stand we have described, whether or not you postpone overtly declaring it. Maximizing love and well-being for one and all, as an alternative to misusing drugs and alcohol, is precisely what this book is about.

We will let you in on a little secret. There are actually no real alternatives to choosing love and well-being—it is only a question of pacing. Our goal is to speed up the process so that you get there before senility sets in.

To do your job properly as manager, you need to determine what is and isn't in alignment with the commitment to love and well-being that you represent. Buddhists call this kind of objective reflection "mindfulness." It generates *detachment,* another word associated with Eastern philosophy. When practiced, it is like being able to step outside of yourself, objectively reflecting on what is going on inside.

We should add that mindfulness and detachment are entirely distinct from suppression and denial. Suppression and denial are attempts to avoid experiencing upsets. Mindfulness and detachment involve acknowledging—staying in touch with—whatever happens, including the good, the bad, and the indifferent. Mindfulness and detachment entail learning to stay centered even in the face of upsets.

The first intent of this exercise is to enhance your ability as manager to be a neutral observer of what goes on inside. We call this gaining *transparency*—the ability to see clearly and honestly what is going on in your heart and mind. We want to cultivate transparency even in connection with the upsetting stuff you previously avoided, buried, built a wall against, or drowned in a chemical soup. For you to govern effectively, you need to become skillful at facing and handling all of it. This is done by learning how to step back and adopt a detached position.

Through the ages, people have effectively used these observation techniques to gain mastery over their lives. What we are doing in the next exercise is opening up these possibilities to you. The rest of the book will be largely about expanding your skill in using these powerful tools.

DISCOVERY 7: Mindfulness and Detachment

In a moment, we will be suggesting that you allow yourself to become attentive to anything that pops into awareness. When you do this, you will probably note that various thoughts and images arise, soon to be swept aside or eclipsed by still other thoughts and images that come drifting through. You may also notice that feelings and sensations ebb and flow—these may be connected with the ongoing stream of ideas or may seem to come from out of the blue.

You do not have to do anything with the thoughts and experiences that appear on your "mind screen." *Just allow them to be there*. When they depart, do not argue with them; just let them go! The idea is to become as objective an observer as you can be of your entire self, the whole mind committee at work and play. And what a show it is! If you discover that one thought or image crowds out another, fine. If the first thought fights back and ends up winning more airtime, fine. Tremendous power can come from developing the skill to view and know yourself in this basically nonevaluative, free-floating way.

As you take a step back and practice observing, you may notice paradoxical ideas, including thoughts such as "I'm not having any thoughts." Or you may discover that thoughts and images arrive unexpectedly from nowhere and then drift away, just as mysteriously, to parts unknown. Thinking is more automatic and less logical than most of us like to believe.

You do not need to figure anything out in order to observe. You will just be lightly and inquisitively looking over your own mental shoulder. Once again, the trick is to *just notice stuff*. The job, for now, has nothing to do with judging or evaluating. Just thank any thought that shows up for having put in an appearance, even if it was not what you expected or might have preferred. In addition to noticing specific thoughts that come and go, you will be observing the fact that thoughts do, in fact, come and go.

Suppose you were to observe thoughts like, "Boy, I don't understand a thing here," "This is stupid," or "I'm just not very bright." Negative stuff like that. Notice that certain members of your internal committee like to generate such thoughts. You do not need to agree with them nor do you need to quibble with them. If they drift through, accept them as legitimate and appropriate to the moment. To repeat a crucial point: The emphasis is on allowing the mental process to proceed and to observe it in progress, in a light and nonjudgmental way. Suppose you notice the thought "I can't do this." No problem. Just sit with the notion that the thought "I can't do this" has grabbed the mike and invaded your personal space. You may also notice thoughts like the following: "Uh-oh, now I'm quibbling with that thought, even though I was warned not to." Simply note that quibbling about quibbling happened and that you felt powerless to do anything about it.

What you will be discovering by becoming a detached observer is your reflective mind at play. It is virtually like stepping outside yourself and peeking in. It is quite amazing (and empowering) once you get the hang of it.

Here's a tip in case you encounter what we call "the Sister Mary complex." Sister Mary was a new nun and, understandably, she really, really wanted to please God. One day she was being such a good nun that she was allowed to bring tea to the Mother Superior—a great, great honor. Everything was going perfectly. The tea service was beautifully arrayed and the sugar and cookies were precisely laid out. Sister Mary took the tray and proudly, devoutly, and gracefully moved into the room. Then, she tripped on the carpet, spilling everything. She automatically cursed: "Oh Christ." Then she swore again: "Oh God, I said Christ! . . . Oh damn, I said God! . . . Oh shit, I said damn!" Get the picture?

To reiterate, the difficult aspect of this discovery exercise is to just notice stuff . . . including noticing that you have stopped noticing. This state can be

hard to achieve, given the automatic attachment we
have to our own thinking and the awesome emotional power it can exert over us.

Do the Following:

Go ahead and spend five minutes observing your
reflective mind in action just the way we have described.

~

How did the exercise go? It might have been difficult this
first time. You might have found yourself getting antsy,
confused, or blocked. You may have become enmeshed,
like Sister Mary, in a spiral of judgments and evaluations,
including appraisals of how well you were doing the exercise. That is to be expected.

Under no circumstances should you give up. There will be
plenty of opportunities to give up later! If you collapsed
due to an intense jumble of negative evaluations (or even
positive ones), just notice that evaluations routinely happen. They are powerful components of normal mind op-
erations. This is the way it is for humans—they make
judgments, and they make judgments about judgments.

Once you gain the ability to just notice the mind committee at play—in effect drifting through judgments and
evaluations—life will start to become a bit less of a burden. When you begin letting go of the hard-core judging
and evaluating that goes on almost continuously in your
mind, you may discover something enormously liberating. You may notice that despite how strong feelings seem
at times, *nothing* is all that important or significant.

Practice Makes Perfect

It is very useful to make the process of lightly observing your thinking into a frequent routine or a daily ritual. Many people practice various forms of such meditation or mindfulness. It keeps them centered, in touch with the flow of life and on guard against the harsh, unloving, and destructive judgments and evaluations that often preoccupy our minds. Much of this book concerns altering a fundamental set of negative beliefs about yourself and life. Mindfulness meditation can be a powerful tool to help you move beyond these negative, demeaning, or arrogant scripts. The suffering some of us endure is not because our minds are filled with beliefs and judgments. The real culprit is the ferocity with which we cling to these self-judgments. Mindfulness and the detachment it brings takes the horror out of our judgments.

You can meditate once or twice a day (during quiet times) or try being mindful for a few seconds right in the middle of other activities. Just have your managerial self in place to notice the flow of thoughts, especially the unloving judgments and evaluations that may frequently invade your day. Notice the ultra-importance you tend to assign to your own pursuits, goals, and expectations. At the same time, gently remind yourself of the fact that *life itself does not seem to care what you do or what you want.* Please note that we are not saying you should give up your goals and expectations. We are simply suggesting that these are important mainly to you—not to the universe as a whole.

Practicing mindfulness allows for powerful detachment. Successful management means gaining the skill to stand back and observe. It is a process of putting some intelligent distance, or perspective, between you and the stuff that can seem overwhelming. Mindful observation permits more graceful acceptance of whatever happens. In the next chapter, we propose a bit of mindful reflection concerning your relationship with drugs and alcohol.

CHAPTER 5

Conversing with Drugs and Alcohol

Unexamined, disempowering beliefs play a large role in limiting your ability to get chemicals out of your system. After all, if you are not in touch with powerful beliefs that are in your mind—and the knowledge that they are *simply beliefs*—how can you effectively deal with them? Building on the mindfulness exercise in the previous chapter, we now ask you, the manager, to come forward and focus your attention on your internal committee's dialogue about drugs and/or alcohol. Perhaps thoughts about such topics dominate your life. Or they may normally hover menacingly in the background of consciousness, poised to disrupt other activities.

We will be asking you to review some specific, perhaps previously unacknowledged opinions that infiltrate your mind space in relationship to mood-altering substances—answers to questions such as "Do you need drugs?" "Do they need you?" "Are they friends? Enemies? Both?" "Having become an integral part of your life, would they be willing to leave if asked politely?" "Do they present themselves as invited guests, unwelcome intruders, or mocking bystanders?" Remember, such questions will be put to the entire committee, with you, as the manager, observing the responses.

We also will be interested in whether there is an "I told you so" personality in the picture, always second-guessing your decisions and actions. Do thoughts and impulses concerning drugs and alcohol sneak up slowly, with plenty of advance warning, or blast through like flash floods or sudden tornadoes, picking up you, the owner, and throwing you about like a small twig? How does the typical drug and alcohol self-conversation begin and end? Is there one hard-and-fast script, or are there a number of variations on the theme?

DISCOVERY 8: Reflecting on Chemical Substances and You

Do the Following:

Take a little time to reflect on your thoughts about these matters. Manager, please notice when you are being sidetracked into taking judgments and evaluations seriously rather than simply noticing lightly what they are. As part of this reflective process, please ask your entire internal self the following questions, letting answers drift in, without pressing for the expression of any particular point of view. Remember, there are no right or wrong answers to these questions. Any answers your mind committee gives will be fine. However, be forewarned that the tenor of the internal discussion may change from moment to moment, as different participants gain the floor.

- How would you describe your relationship to your drug of choice?
- How do you and that drug get along? Are you friends or combatants? Do you do that drug, or does it do you?
- How does this drug treat you? (Tell the whole story about this to yourself, not just the politically correct one. Remember, people use drugs and alcohol because they produce results experienced as preferable to being clean and sober!)
- What does the drug generally say to you, and what is your most typical answer? What is its answer to your answer?
- What rights and privileges does the drug claim to have? What rights, if any, do you have in the matter? (It is okay if these questions produce the same, similar, or contradictory answers.)

~

As you attempted to simply observe the answers that arose in response to these questions, was there one rascal of a participant who seemed a little overeager to end the exercise? Did that character try to convince you—the manager—that this was all just a waste of time? Did he or she claim that you already knew what you thought about such matters? Was the entire gang up there happy to pack it in and return to the TV? Did you, being the dedicated leader that you are, persist anyway? Alas, we must ask: Were you even on the job?

Perhaps you dropped the ball and didn't even do the previous discovery exercise. Perhaps an internal voice convinced you that it was not really necessary (in your particular case). Perhaps it argued that it was beneath you to slavishly follow someone else's stupid instructions. As we all know, instructions are mainly for others who aren't as clever as we are.

Now we'd like you to repeat the same exercise again. However, pretend it is one year from now. What would you, as manager, dearly like the answers to those questions to be? We are not asking for a prediction. Nobody owns a crystal ball. We are just asking that you, as manager, confirm for yourself where you would like to be headed regarding your relationship with drugs and alcohol.

Specifying your heartfelt desires in relation to drugs and alcohol, or other vital issues, is apt to be scary. Nobody likes to fail in relation to something that really matters. However, a burning desire is an important tool in getting to where one wants to go. Used properly, it counteracts all the negative stuff that keeps you stuck. You are being invited to give voice to desire as an inspirational and motivational tool, not as a predictor of the future. When you have finished doing the exercise above using the "one year later" perspective, we will be ready to continue.

Now that you, as manager, have had some experience doing these exercises, we have something essential for you to really cut your teeth on. Keep yourself particularly open, sharp, and clear, and make sure you are in front of the pack. If you have been taking a nap, wake up, because it is you we are relying on to carry this project through to completion.

A Proof of Innocence

We suspect that within your mind's committee there are intense inner conversations about guilt and shame, particularly in connection with the misuse of chemicals. Contrary to conventional wisdom, however, *heavy guilt and shame serve no useful function*. As psychiatrist Ron Smothermon puts it, if you cease doing something harmful in a condition of guilt, "it is *despite* the guilt, not because of it" (emphasis added, 1980, p. 19). Guilty feelings have a tendency to keep us stuck, unable to effectively clean up our act and live productively. To the outside world, guilt appears to motivate reform, but to the scoundrels on the mind's executive committee it just paves the way for repeating whatever it is we happen to feel guilty about. In the convoluted logic of the mind, paying for misdeeds through guilt makes it easier for additional transgressions to occur. As Smothermon notes, guilt becomes part of a vicious trespass-guilt-trespass-guilt cycle.

Because beating yourself up for presumed sins doesn't do any good, we recommend that you urge the internal mental committee to get out of the guilt racket—lock, stock, and barrel. If you are going to harm or invalidate yourself or others, you might as well do it *responsibly*, without hiding behind the protective screen that being shamefaced provides. Contrary to what all of us have been taught, guilt plays no constructive role in preventing the recurrence of negative deeds.

The idea that people should consider themselves bad and sinful derives from the assumption that if they had been more careful or had tried harder, they could have avoided most of life's misfortunes. We disagree. Heaping blame on yourself for past deeds does little except pave the way for additional calamities. People who feel blame-worthy *expect* things to go wrong, and life has a tendency to fulfill their expectations. In other words, individuals who consider themselves losers usually continue doing what losers do best. That way they at least get to be right about their predictions.

The perspective from which self-designated losers listen to the world practically guarantees a succession of disasters. From our point of view, they would be much better off if they would shuck—once and for all—the whole guilt-loser-blame cycle.

DISCOVERY 9: A Heart of Innocence

As an aid in helping you, as manager, shake your entire system loose from unproductive cycles of self-condemnation, we want to hammer away at a point we touched upon in an earlier chapter—your essential innocence. This time around we invite you, the leader of the executive committee, to seriously ponder the following question: At what *precise point* does a person who begins life as an innocent baby become tainted, smudged by sin, and thereafter deserving of punishment and condemnation from self and others? When, exactly—on what day, at what moment, in what precise nanosecond—is purity and innocence lost? When does an individual begin choosing to do the wrong thing, thus transforming himself or herself from guileless innocent to culpable villain? After you have thought about that question for a few moments, continue reading.

Most of us grew up in the presence of reproachful adults who, while battling their own guilt, waved a scornful finger at us at every misstep. They implied that we could and should have done the right thing but instead willfully chose to misbehave, disobey, or flout the rules. Condemned to our room, to the principal's office, or to the county jail, we uttered a rebellious "fuck you" or its equivalent, pretending that their appraisals didn't really matter to us. Not permitted to go on an outing, we rationalized that it would have been a stupid trip anyway. Society is arranged so that there is almost always a judgmental axe ready to fall. Furthermore, after a series of ugly incidents, many of us actually position ourselves under precariously perched weaponry, thereby wresting at least a measure of control and predictability from an apparently indifferent or hostile world.

Of course, bouts of self-reproach might make sense if it could be proven that those adults were right—that we literally *chose* to screw up. On the other hand, if it could be shown that we never messed up on purpose or of our own accord, we would remain essentially innocent souls. In other words, if it can be demonstrated that we are not literally guilty of anything, then a central aspect of the context in which we live our lives might shift dramatically. The future would seem less burdensome.

We would be freed from continually having to either admit to being guilty losers or having to prove that we are now, finally, doing our damndest to reform.

Before we continue this discovery exercise, check and make sure that you—as manager—are securely strapped in the pilot's seat. Remember, you are the one who was designated to develop a strong commitment to maximize compassion and well-being. Listen especially for any of the regular naysayers, including those who seem to represent judgmental parents, spouses, offspring, outside authorities, and so on. We are about to invite you alone to be the judge and jury concerning the innocence or guilt of your whole being.

To have all the facts necessary to arrive at an informed verdict, we will need to go way back to the beginning . . . before you as a person were even a twinkle in your mother's eye. So, imagine a time before you were born. You were in that great empty nowhere. It might help to imagine that you were just a possibility waiting in the wings, somewhere, in a vast space that we will call "no place in particular."

Into that absolutely peaceful emptiness where you were comfortably nestled, a message rang out, in the voice of God, or Mother Nature, asking: "Want to put in an appearance on Earth? Want to be born?

"You have a choice here, of course. This is a democratic system. You can stay peacefully where you are or you can become a human being. Perhaps you would rather be born some other sort of creature or plant. Would you prefer to be a rock, an idea, a tide, a bookmark?"

Notice that in this fantasy reenactment, we describe your imminent appearance on this planet as a distinct set of choices. In actuality, nothing could be further from the truth. Actually, you were never consulted in the matter. Was anyone even the tiniest bit interested in your opinion at this most critical juncture, the beginning of your existence? We think not! "Oh, by the way, here's the thing about being human. You will suffer more or less throughout life. You might get lucky and become one of the very few who go from victory to victory. In the end, however, you will still lose everything you love, shriveling up and dying, perhaps at a most inopportune moment. Sound good? What do you say? Wanna play?"

Well, despite the obvious hazards, you might have voted for such an opportunity, if you had been given an informed choice. But, you were not! That single fact, that *there was no choice involved whatsoever,* makes a huge difference in terms of your essential guilt or innocence. It makes a difference in terms of whether you deserve to suffer and continue being a willing participant in the game of guilt.

But, let's not stop here at birth. There are so many additional choices to be considered. How about gender? After all, there is a big difference between being born a man or a woman! "Oh yes, there is this other little matter," Mother Nature might have said. "You can be born either male or female. Okay, here's the difference . . ." Of course, after the difference was fully explained, you would have made your decision, perhaps using the latest computer technology to weigh the relevant factors, all with

your eyes fully open to the various perils and poten-
tialities.

Again, note that you were given no say about
your gender, nor about your place of birth, parents,
body type, hair color, intelligence level, athletic
prowess, musical aptitude, and so on. We could go
on and on with this hypothetical exercise, but the
point would remain the same: When it comes to any
of the basics that make a difference, there was absolutely no choice.

In fact, if you take away everything that makes
us *us* that we did not ask for or select, what is left?
If everything that makes us who we are—our humanity, genetic makeup, country of origin, cultural
environment, and so on—has been predetermined
and foisted on us without consultation, there is certainly nothing left to be guilty about! How could there
be? We have, in each and every moment of our existence, simply been doing what we have been designed and programmed to do, reacting to the
events we bump into as best we knew how in a cu-
mulative and endless progression. Incidentally, this
is what biologists call "natural drift."

Let's coolly reflect on this highly unusual situation, Mr. or Ms. Manager. Upon deep reflection, we
simply appear to be products of a set of creative or
haphazard forces that go back beyond the beyond.
Even our thoughts just tumble out and announce
themselves in response to whatever is happening.
Now, unless you can find some loophole in this logic
and identify some truly independent contribution

you made to the matter of your being, we suggest that you give up on guilt altogether.

If your current behavior seems preferable to your past behavior, then please just accept that fortuitous improvement gracefully, without presuming that guilt somehow produced it. As we have said, most of the time guilt does little more than sustain a belief in an outmoded logic of false causes—the notion that we are self-contained units who operate independently of our biological machinery and surrounding environmental forces.

You have undoubtedly lived with guilt and shame long enough for you, as manager, to see how useless it is in generating healthy and satisfying options. If guilt and punishment really worked as advertised, then we would have fewer criminals returning to jail and fewer binge eaters marching off with a tub of ice cream while, at the same time, being fully aware they are setting themselves up for a bout of self-condemnation.

We are reminded of a former client who, having landed in jail, swore up and down that when he was released, he would never go back to a life of crime. He was enormously guilt-ridden and convinced himself that he had finally learned his lesson. However, a savvy repeat offender, hearing him talk about the depths of his regrets, sidled up to him and said, "You sound like me, when I was in for the first time!"

We know that you may have done some pretty awful things in your lifetime. That is not the point. Had you been born a cat, the worst you might have done is scratched the furniture or dispatched a few birds. However, human beings are capable of a much broader range of mischief. Still, the process by which cats and humans "sin" is essentially the same. Fortunately, cats do not do much philosophizing about it. (Otherwise, we might have to listen to them sermonize about "going straight" in between sparrow hunts.)

By now, some inner voice may be saying, "But if I am not to blame for my behavior—not guilty, no matter what—why should I do the right thing?" Interestingly, when self-acceptance is high, people tend to do their best naturally, and they are generally attentive to the rights and needs of others. People who know themselves as innocents turn out to be pretty decent citizens. The rules of the community work most smoothly when people are not feeling pressed to justify and defend their worth—when their personal survival does not seem to be under constant threat. Under those circumstances, the ordinary consequences of social interaction (which apply whether or not we are ultimately innocent) are sufficient to keep us on track.

So, here is the question, Mr. or Ms. Manager: Given the preceding information, see if you are willing to accept that logically all of us—including you—are innocent of all charges. We are not truly, literally, really, guilty of the miserable things we may have done, including, perhaps, repetitive acts of self-destruction. Therefore, we are entitled to begin the process of giving ourselves a break. What do you think? Yes or no? As manager of the executive committee, having reviewed the evidence, do you agree that it is futile to keep indulging in uncompassionate blame, guilt, and shame?

Our thesis is that these are the emotional states that keep the mind stuck in misery and, paradoxically, amplify cravings for drugs and alcohol and a variety of other mischievous substances. Thus, these emotions contribute to perpetuating the very irresponsibility they appear designed to curb. If you agree, it will be your job to notice when the shame game starts up again and how convincing the negative arguments of certain internal committee members sound. Becoming aware of these repetitive patterns loosens their grip on the system. After awhile, the rantings of the mind demons will begin to seem tired and hackneyed. Under those conditions, guilt will cease to be an effective saboteur.

As a compassionate manager, see if you are willing to stand guard, ready to take on those logical sounding—but ultimately fallacious—voices of shame, blame, self-recrimination, and accusation. If not, simply note that you still find the internal voices of guilt and shame compelling. We will provide several more opportunities to examine this issue in later chapters.

~

In the next chapter, we discuss an aspect of guilt that may still be of concern: responsibility for one's actions. For many people, throwing out guilt is synonymous with giving up on responsibility. We offer a different perspective on the matter.

CHAPTER 6

Attaining Balance

If, in the previous chapter, you were able to loosen your attachment to hard-core guilt and are becoming more accustomed to asserting your essential innocence in all things, it makes sense to return to the matter of accountability. This gets to the heart of "the middle way"—a Buddhist philosophy that preaches straddling apparently contradictory notions. In this case, the notions are that (a) life is not your fault, and (b) you are fully responsible for all of your actions. On the one hand, you are automatically and unconditionally granted a heart of innocence. On the other hand, you are invited to play the game of life with skill and power by becoming accountable for the effects you produce.

The paradox partially disappears when you realize that we are not using words like *responsibility* or *accountability* as synonyms for blame or praise. It would be foolish to blame water for running downstream or to yell at it for being so doggedly gravitational. Yet, a person building an irrigation system needs to carefully take into account the principles of hydrodynamics. Similarly, accountability and

responsibility—as we use the terms—involve acknowledging and appreciating who we are—biologically and
psychologically—and using that information to advance
our goals. The goal is to produce results, not to recrim-
inate ourselves or others with moral invectives.

We have already demonstrated that if you go back to
ground zero, you can see that you were not given a vote
about anything. Your life experiences are yours merely
because you happen to be standing in the middle of them.
Let us put it as simply as we can: The stork somehow
magically plucked you out of nothingness and dropped
you into a particular place with a particular bundle of
biological and psychological equipment. From that point
forward, off you went, playing out the hand you were
dealt.

To experience satisfaction and well-being, you need to
play that hand enthusiastically and skillfully without
spending a lot of time criticizing the cards you hold. The
paradoxical stance of basic innocence *and* maximum accountability provides an ideal position from which to enjoy the game. It takes the horror out of those everyday
dramas that toss us back and forth between bouts of pride
and shame, praise and condemnation.

Through a willingness to be responsible for your
actions—by saying "the buck stops here"—you nourish
the best in yourself and enhance your sense of personal
authority. A powerful CEO takes full responsibility for
ensuring customer satisfaction even though he or she may
not even have been in charge when the glitch being complained about occurred. Again, *blame* and *responsibility*, as
we use the terms, are not synonymous.

Note that what we are discussing is not based on or

compatible with ordinary logic. However, modern science urges us to view the world holistically—a position that often forces us to transcend black-and-white alternatives. For instance, scientists now know that destroying a nuisance species can have unforeseen and distressing effects on the larger ecology. Insects or bacteria that seem to be enemies may, in the final analysis, turn out to be friends. In today's world, the truth often seems more paradoxical than straightforward. The physicists tell us light is neither a wave nor a particle—it is both. Moreover, it was recently reported that physicists have created an atom that can exist in two places *at the same time*. Go figure.

Living the middle way—the key to enlightenment—can be thought of as surmounting apparent paradoxes by using two different parts of our brains at virtually the same time. In Mode No. 1, we appreciate the conventional wisdom with which we wake each morning and tackle breakfast. In Mode No. 2, we employ a special intuitive, holistic outlook that is easier to grasp than explain. In Mode No. 1, you clumsily spilled the glass of orange juice. In Mode No. 2, you recognize that the configuration of the universe makes juice spilling more or less inevitable. In Mode No. 1, life appears to be a tumultuous chessboard, where game pieces vie for dominance and control. In Mode No. 2, we hover above the board, where we can enjoy the fascination of the game and appreciate the close interrelationships among the pieces. In order to maximize compassion and well-being, your manager needs to become adept at juggling these two different but complementary perspectives.

Balancing such opposites is a bit like walking a tightrope or riding a bicycle. If you go too far in any one direction, you fall. However, if you oscillate or fluctuate from side to side, you stay upright. Enlightenment is the psychological and emotional equivalent of bike riding. A smooth passage is achieved by rocking constantly between contradictory postures. In Mode No. 1, it is sensible to play hard in a game—as if it was serious and your entire being depended on the outcome. At the same time, the Mode No. 2 perspective urges us to remember that it is only a game and has no ultimate importance.

Actually, we heartily recommend viewing life as a series of games. When you are in the midst of one of these games, play full out. At the same time, keep in mind that there are no final winners or losers. Think about it: This is how small children operate. When they are playing, the game becomes their whole world. A moment later the game is forgotten and they are on to their next adventure. They fall down, scrape a knee, cry their hearts out, and recover practically instantaneously. Important, not important, important, not important. The cosmic joke is that whether saint or sinner, king or commoner, success or failure, we are all headed for exactly the same place.

We are not asking that you fully understand the concepts we have just outlined. If you do, so much the better. If not, just hang in there and float lightly in the sea of confusion. As any Zen or Taoist master will tell you, confusion is a very high state—it signals that something new and interesting is underway. It is when you think you know it all and are unwilling to tolerate uncertainty, that you inhibit new learning. Recall how mysterious bike riding seemed at first until that instant when it suddenly, unexpectedly came together for you. What power and freedom resides in that moment!

Two last thoughts before we end this chapter: If you—
as manager—accept yourself as innocent, because logically
you cannot see how you objectively asked for a life of
misery, then consistency dictates that you grant the same
ultimate innocence to everybody else, including those vil-
lainous souls who, according to your mind committee,
"did it to you." Remember, in Mode No. 2 they are
simply part of how the universe is constructed.

Now would be a good time to forget everything that
we have said thus far and grant yourself a brief vacation.
We have been putting information into the living computer of your brain. It will work its magic more or less
automatically. When you feel up to it, turn to the next
chapter, where we continue to attempt to motivate and
clarify your quest for a life of compassion and well-being
without drugs.

CHAPTER 7

Revitalizing Desire

In this chapter, we further pound away at the twin issues of guilt and shame. We attempt to neutralize any committee members who insist that life be a losing proposition for you. We want to help rejuvenate your zest for living.

Most of us are born raring to go. Yet, by the time we are teens, many of us have lost our edge and have begun to feel angry, downtrodden, or defeated. In response, we are apt to develop either an excessively cautious, avoidant approach to life or a rebellious, who-gives-a-damn attitude.

Carl Rogers, the well-known humanistic psychologist, noted that by the age of two, most children have been pummeled by what he called "conditions of worth." We go from not being able to do anything wrong, to not being able to do much right. "No, you can't run over your baby sister with your Big Wheel!" "No, putting the fork in the light socket is *definitely* a bad idea!" In some families, a *smack* punctuates these verbal admonitions. As these unpleasant clashes with reality mount up, youngsters sometimes conclude that there is something drastically wrong with them, with others, or with life itself.

Unfortunately, school often adds to children's growing sense of frustration. Bursting at the seams with energy and aliveness, they are ordered, on pain of visiting the principal's office, to sit still, be quiet, and follow orders. This is a five-day-a-week, six-hour-a-day, ten-months-a-year regimen. We are not commenting on whether or not the educational system should be changed. We are simply describing how many children perceive their school experience.

At the same time, kids may encounter the sting of peer rejection. Youngsters tend to be even more fickle and ruthless than adults when it comes to being harshly judgmental. "Oooh, look at the geek!" children will say of a person with the wrong looks, the wrong interests, or even the wrong sneakers. Our point is that few of us make it through childhood unscathed. For a substantial number, it is a calamitous journey.

As a result of childhood experiences, virtually all of us accumulate a stockpile of self-deprecatory characterizations. Periodically, we recite these to ourselves, keeping them alive well beyond the time period during which they were initially uttered. Such bouts of self-condemnation emanate from, and strengthen the hand of, the negative members of our internal mental committee.

In the last chapter, we argued for your essential innocence. However, that general declaration may not have been sufficient to fend off the frequent insurrections of internal guilt-mongers. In order to gain the upper hand, your manager needs to be fully conversant with their bag of tricks and practiced at mounting an effective counter-attack.

Note, first of all, that the barbs of negative committee members are highly repetitive. Not particularly inventive, they harp on the same points, over and over again. You can rest assured that even when their rants appear to be novel, they are basically the same tired grumblings, gussied up to fit current circumstances. In fact, negative internal committee members can rarely dredge up more than three or four basic flaws to complain about. Through relentless repetition, they get maximum mileage from a limited arsenal of grievances.

Keep in mind that negative committee members are convinced they are doing you a favor by reminding you of your faults. Yet, their monotonous drumbeat serves mainly to kill desire and dampen enthusiasm for healthy change. Constant self-criticism leads to depression, not growth.

We offer the next exercise as an opportunity to focus on exactly the kinds of assertions internal mind demons carp about. By being crystal clear about how the negative committee members operate, your manager will be better equipped to survive both frontal assaults and sneak attacks.

DISCOVERY 10: Identifying Mental Banditos

Manager, please start a list on paper of familiar self-reproaches and complaints heaped upon you by certain nasty *banditos* on your mind's committee. Include everything that comes to mind. Don't stint

and don't be concerned about repeating yourself—
if the mental banditos can do it, so can you. If you
think two items are basically the same, put both of
them down anyway. We are aiming for complete-
ness. Resist any tendency to dismiss, censure, excuse, minimize, or apologize. This is not about trying
to look good. Don't quibble with your mind. If something pops up, put it down. Add items to the list even
if they seem illogical, false, or exaggerated. Bum
raps count.

Now, go back and see if you can make some of
the items more specific. Exactly what are the accusations of those internal committee members in
charge of guilt and shame? What are their favorite
forms of character assassination? Which of your
traits do they despise? What do they say you have
done to yourself or others that is especially blame-
worthy? How, in their view, have you detracted from
the health, well-being, or satisfaction of friends, relatives, and loved ones? Why do they keep insisting
that you do not deserve to be happy and successful?
What, in their view, warrants your continued suffering and failure? Why are they nominating you for
president of the local (or national) losers' club? As
you examine each of those questions, add items to
your list that you might not otherwise have thought
of, and continue reviewing and clarifying the items
that are there.

Now, to complete your list, acknowledge any
other reasons that appear to make you so damna-
ble. What have you done (or might you still be doing)
that gives credence to the refrain of those guilt-

mongers in your mind? Perhaps, unconsciously, you have bypassed some ugly self-truths that you do not want to face. Return to the list and come clean about these. The goal in this exercise is to present the vilest self-portrait possible. Let's get it out there and be done with it.

~

Having looked over this list of accusations, it is time to reflect logically on why you did, and perhaps continue to do, things that are destructive to yourself or others. It is time to begin refuting the false reasoning that keeps you stuck in anger, frustration, and despair. As we stated earlier, there are always perfectly valid reasons for all of our behaviors. By the end of this book you will see, with great clarity, that in every situation you were indeed innocent at heart and at every step of the way you did exactly what you had to do given the circumstances you were facing.

This idea of perfect innocence may still seem quite radical to you. We know that you are likely to continue to feel on shaky ground in spite of everything we have been saying about it. Most people do not understand this stance and would accuse you of just making excuses or justifying self-indulgence. We are definitely urging a position that runs counter to some of our culture's most time-honored traditions. However, traditional views often keep people stuck. Progress requires breaking free from the conventional wisdom.

In the next chapter we will be asking you to examine some of the reasons for your "wicked ways"—the transgressions you listed in the previous exercise. First, however, we want to share Ted's story. It represents an extreme situation, but many of you will identify with his basic experiences.

Ted's Story

Ted was fifteen. His addiction to crack cocaine was severe enough to land him in a residential drug-treatment program for teens. (One of the authors was his counselor.) To obtain money for his habit, Ted would routinely engage in crime. His mother had given up on trying to control him, and residential treatment was seen as his last hope of avoiding incarceration. Oddly enough, Ted was a very polite, cooperative—even sweet—youngster. He hardly fit the stereotype of a recalcitrant delinquent.

Ted's mom was a nice and loving lady. She tried to steer Ted in the right direction, but she had problems of her own. She had been sexually molested as a child by her drunken father, and most of the men she chose to love drank too much and used drugs and their fists too freely. Ted's mother felt profoundly weak and unable to cope with life. Naturally, as children, Ted and his younger sister were ill-equipped to prevent the painful chaos that chronically infected their household. To make matters worse, Ted's biological father, James, had sexually molested both him and his sister from the time she was two and he was four.

While Ted was at the treatment center, his dad was just getting out of jail. He had been convicted of child abuse but also had a prior police record of drunken assaults and driving under the influence. He claimed, however, that the treatment he received in prison allowed him to come to terms with his "sickness." As part of the family counseling offered at the center, Ted was asked if he would like to meet with his father. It would certainly have been understandable if he had declined. However, both he and his father readily agreed. When they met, Ted sat quietly while his father recounted harrowing aspects of his own childhood.

Ted's grandparents had been musicians. They lived in rural Quebec. They would often spend weekends away from the family at various gigs. On these occasions, James would usually be parked at the home of his mother's unmarried sister. When he was about eight, James's parents died tragically in an automobile crash while on one of their road trips. To add to the misfortune, his aunt announced that she was unable to care for James on a full-time basis. He was thus sent away to Montreal for foster care.

James recounted that both his foster father and his foster mother sexually molested him. By the age of thirteen, he had become a rebellious youngster who smoked, drank, and was frequently truant. Perhaps because of his defiant behavior, he was eventually transferred to an orphanage run by Catholic brothers, several of whom also molested him sexually.

Of course, this was during an era when there was little public discussion about the sexual abuse of children in families and institutions—it was pre-Oprah. Because of this lack of awareness, pedophilic individuals often became foster parents in order to gain sexual access to vulnerable children.

Ted sat and listened silently, seemingly unmoved by his father's narrative and his plea to be forgiven for his own familial transgressions. We wish we could report that this aspect of the story had a happy ending—that the two reconciled. Perhaps some day they will reconcile. However, the truth is that following that session, Ted refused to have anything further to do with his father. His sister, on the other hand, was more forgiving and has, as far as we know, maintained a good relationship with James.

One last tragic twist to the tale: Before Ted left the center, he revealed that he too was attracted to young children and had fantasized about having sex with them. The staff thought it likely that such activity had already taken place.

The question is: *Just whom do we blame for Ted's problems?* Do we blame dad? Child molesters are certainly among the most villainized citizens these days. Yet, as we saw, Ted's dad claims to have been driven, in large part, by the abuse that he himself suffered. Furthermore, there is now credible scientific evidence that pedophilic urges—like many other sexual proclivities—have genetic links and are among the most difficult patterns to tame or change. Perhaps the blame lies with Ted's mom, who chose his dad as a mate in the first place and did little to shield her children from him. What kind of mother would do that? But she might not have known what was going on, and even if she did, she might not have had the physical, psychological, and financial resources to effectively curb or confront her husband's behavior. Again, in those days, there was not much support for wives who wanted to oppose their husband's misbehavior.

Maybe we should blame the authorities. In hindsight, they did not do nearly enough to protect the helpless children in their charge. But, most administrators of that period were quite naïve about what went on behind closed doors. Moreover, the power hierarchy and cultural climate combined to stifle protests from individual employees. Of course, the perpetrators themselves probably all had stories as compelling as those told by Ted and James—they grew up in dysfunctional environments, struggling against insistent biological urges. To find the first cause of Ted's dilemmas, we might have to go way back to the cave dwellers, Og and Oog. However, Og and Oog would undoubtedly claim that they were just doing what came naturally, behaving the way cave folk had for generations.

At first blush, none of this seems very satisfying. As humans, we like to be able to assign blame. When we feel serious wrongs have been committed we want to find and punish a transgressor or be able to condemn a group for being evil or indifferent. Our system of law and order is based on the premise that for every misdeed, a person or institution can be singled out and considered culpable. However, to make that system work, we are forced to selectively overlook any information that would portray perpetrators in a sympathetic light.

In court cases, a jury that operates according to community standards generally establishes legal accountability. However, science has long since outstripped the commonsense views of the man on the street. The culture may still insist on simplistic distinctions between badness and madness, condemnation and sympathy. However, these divisions can no longer be scientifically defended. For instance, it is currently fashionable to demonize serial killers and other psychopaths because of their heinous crimes and the fact that they show so little remorse. Yet, there is good evidence that the acts of such individuals represent the end result of unfortunate genetic patterns often exacerbated by family instability and communal break-down. Public condemnation will do little to improve their plight or insure the welfare of future generations of potential victims. Reducing psychopathy requires enlightened social policy coupled with creative research.

Over time, the justice system changes. We no longer stone adulterers, throw the inebriated into prison, or burn psychotic "witches" at the stake. However, the culture develops slowly, and we are still stuck with the remnants of a basically outmoded system of causal analysis in which we arbitrarily condemn some people and exonerate others.

Note that although we argue that no one is to blame—or, conversely, that everyone is equally culpable—we are not suggesting that dangerous criminals be allowed to walk the streets or that muggings be tolerated. Citizens have a right to be protected, and it is legitimate for societies to develop and enforce a code of conduct. However, labeling particular individuals malevolent goes beyond what is necessary to maintain law and order. In fact, identifying individuals as demonic simply breeds additional hatred and misunderstanding, complicating behavioral control for both the violator and the community.

Once we get past our usual angry, self-righteous positions, it becomes apparent that there are always legitimate reasons for people's actions. Once we start searching for ultimate reasons and causes, we are forced to go back through the generations, ending up in a pointless black hole of infinite regression, where every perceived cause is preceded by another perceived cause. Manager, take note: If you were able to view the entirety of anybody's life, frame-by-frame on three-dimensional video, the reasons for people's behavior would become relatively transparent. Given the interplay of nature and nurture, nobody truly earns either sainthood or damnation, credit or blame—step-by-step, people simply are who they are and do what they do.

We have spent a good deal of time creating the grounds for unconditional compassion because of its importance in weakening the unhealthy grip of the guilty mind bandito. In the next chapter, we guide you through an examination of some of your own transgressions from this compassionate viewpoint.

CHAPTER 8

Reexamining Transgressions

Building on our discussion in the previous chapter, we are about to ask you to come up with some sound reasons for your various "sins." You don't have to launch an exhaustive search for explanations—just go into enough detail to establish that you, like everyone else, have been following life's dictates. We want you to solidify for yourself the idea that there are indeed reasonable motivations for your actions. We are looking for logical reasons for your behavior from an environmental and biological perspective.

Biological stuff includes having been a spirited or hyperactive child who had difficulty sitting still, or having been born shy, thereby making it difficult to meet people or enjoy social interaction. Perhaps you were sickly as a youngster or were handicapped by a learning disability. Perhaps you were poorly coordinated and couldn't keep up in sports. Perhaps you were scrawny or chubby, particularly plain or unusually attractive. Perhaps your body chemistry was genetically primed to respond powerfully to addictive substances.

On the environmental front, you might have been raised in poverty or reared in a rough neighborhood. Perhaps, while still a child, you were forced to care for younger siblings or helped take care of a mentally or physically disabled parent. Perhaps you suffered the effects of parental neglect or outright child abuse. Perhaps your talents—musical, artistic, mechanical, literary, athletic— went unrecognized or unappreciated. Perhaps you felt forced to keep up with a fast-living crowd, where boozing was the norm. Perhaps your first introduction to drugs was connected with sports training.

It is now time to look at reasons for your actions. What you are about to do will help strengthen your compassionate self, ultimately profiting everyone, yourself and those around you. So, your manager needs to be on the alert, ready to diminish the grip of your most sinister mind demons.

DISCOVERY 11: Transgression Inventory

Take out your list of felonious and sinful actions— the one you prepared for the discovery exercise in the previous chapter. For each item, provide a few of the biological and environmental reasons that made each event likely, perhaps inevitable. You might want to jot down some marginal notes on your original list, indicating reasons for each behavior that you now regard as an unfortunate lapse of judgment or worse.

Don't worry that some of your mind demons continue to insist that these explanations are merely excuses. Remind those spoilsports that such "excuses" have already won major support from the most enlightened segment of the scientific community. In other words, scientists have known for decades that only nature and nurture drive our behavior. There is no all-knowing homunculus who plotted your downfall and has therefore earned your retribution.

~

The bottom line is that as reason supplants hard-core guilt and shame, positive energy returns, making it easier to live enthusiastically, as well as morally and ethically. When you appreciate your own fundamental innocence, you gain the power to tell your loser banditos to get lost.

Here is another person's tale that we want to bring to your attention in connection with the issues of blame, guilt, and sin.

Laura's Story

Laura is a twenty-year-old client of one of the authors. Her mother sought advice from our center when her daughter started to use heroin. Laura's dad had died suddenly five years earlier, and her mother reported that she had suffered a six-month nervous breakdown. Laura had taken her dad's death very hard, but she wasn't very vocal about her grief. At the time, the focus of everyone's concern was her mother. However, just as her mother seemed to be returning to normal, Laura began acting out at home and at school. Eventually, she began to use heroin.

At her mother's urging, Laura reluctantly agreed to come in for counseling. She was scared and upset, and with good reason. By that point, she had been snorting heroin for about six months and had recently begun skin popping—using needles intramuscularly. She was terrified that she would not be able to stop before graduating to full-blown intravenous use. A shy and sensitive youngster, Laura had always had difficulty expressing her needs to others. Shortly before her father's death, with fights between her parents escalating, she felt lost, anxious, disconnected, and profoundly unhappy.

Laura was a virgin until the age of seventeen, in spite of having become a bit wild in other respects. She explained she was taught to prize her virginity and to deeply value sex as a reflection of love in a relationship. She recalled through tears that one night she and a friend had been drinking and were picked up by two young men in their early twenties. The long and short of it is that she was raped by one of them. Her response—difficult even for Laura to explain—was to begin dating the very man who raped her!

When that relationship broke up, Laura concluded that she was a slut, and she became increasingly promiscuous. She could recount exactly how many men she had slept with in a three-year period, and she reported that just the day before our interview, she had been stoned at a party and offered oral sex to a complete stranger. Laura felt extraordinarily ashamed of her behavior.

Laura had an interesting answer for those who wondered why she continued to see the person who originally raped her: By dating him, she hoped to convince herself that it had not really been rape. Her fervent desire to remain pure drove her toward greater promiscuity. Her behavior may not seem logical when viewed in the cold, harsh light of day, but individuals often engage in tortured mental gymnastics in their valiant attempts to hold on to a prized identity that is slipping away. By the time her relationship with this man ended six months later, she had decided with a vengeance that she was a shameful person who deserved whatever mistreatment she received. Heroin use fit her image of a fallen woman—and at the same time decreased the anguish of that painful self-characterization. Sometimes she felt that if she contracted AIDS in the process, it would be a fitting punishment for her fall from grace. She also fantasized about dying of a drug overdose, thereby putting a quick end to her misery.

Laura's vicious cycle of shame, drugs, and sex was at first difficult to interrupt. She could not give herself a break. She understood the essential innocence of her little sister, and even of some friends who had gone through similar struggles. However, she thought of her own case as different. The majority opinion within her internal committee was that she was, as she claimed, "a hopeless junkie slut." Of course, her willingness to talk to a counselor suggested that not all committee members subscribed to that verdict. Her counselor's stance was to help those minority members find their voice. Laura was genuinely intrigued that someone—anyone—could still perceive her as being pure as the driven snow, given the clear evidence of her "dirty" doings. According to Laura, this show of relentless faith enabled her internal manager to argue for forgiveness and mount a campaign to get her behavior back on track.

The Hopelessness Monster

When negative members of the mind committee team up, the individual voices of guilt, shame, and loss combine to create a malicious hopelessness monster. The growls of this mental Godzilla frequently drown out more positive and reasonable voices.

David's Story

David, one of the authors, has his own hopelessness story. After quitting drugs, and with his life in an absolute mess, David was confronting not only the long-term consequences of his drug use but also the immediate discomforts of withdrawal. With no sense of continuity between the past, the present, and the future, he considered committing himself to a mental institution. Although he normally adores food (and weighs 170 pounds today), his weight had dropped precipitously to 115 pounds. He had no appetite and was existing in a constant state of anxiety and panic. Given his massive confusion about almost everything, he found himself thinking of his anemia as a kind of fashion statement. Loss of appetite gradually transformed itself into anorexia, with David contemplating having a twenty-six-inch waist and being able to fit into his wife's jeans—a goal that at the time seemed strangely alluring but now makes no sense at all.

Years went by, and because David did not seek help, his mental state and outlook further deteriorated. He was suicidal, off and on. On one bleak occasion, he planned to rent a Porsche, take it out on a mountain road, and, with a slight twist of the wheel, rocket off into oblivion. His friends were getting weary of his grim rhetoric—he never had anything positive to say. Indeed, he told everyone within earshot that life was essentially meaningless and corrupt. His wife, at her wit's end, left him, providing further justification for him to rehearse his poor David routine—self-righteous and miserable.

On one fortunate day, David enrolled in a self-help workshop. The leader argued, as we have been arguing here, that from a universal perspective, there is really no point to life. The leader claimed to be teaching the participants about the road to enlightenment. Because David was feeling exceptionally bleak at the time, his hand shot up and he informed the leader that he already knew all about Zen and Buddhism, and that these philosophies had not been of the slightest help. (In retrospect, this was an interesting statement, because it represented one of David's first actual admissions that he needed help.)

The leader accused David of using ancient wisdom to support his own sense of nihilism. He noted that David not only believed his life to be hopeless but also had a stake in insuring that others would come to the same conclusion. David's pattern was to put down anyone who seemed happy or content, maintaining that they were simply foolish and naïve.

The image David attempted to convey was that of a hippie hero, alerting the world to its inherent corruption, using drugs as a symbol of rebellion, and feeling somewhat virtuous in having dropped out (this was during the sixties and seventies). However, soon after the workshop, something the leader had said clicked, and David realized that he was not actually the courageous messenger he envisioned himself to be. In fact, his act was a total sham. This new acknowledgment was initially devastating. Yet, he realized how much unnecessary pain he was in and how much his behavior during the previous decade had hurt those close to him. It took several more years for him to convince his wife that it was safe for her to return. His interaction with the leader clarified the degree to which he had been in the grip of the hopelessness demon. Armed with that insight, he tutored himself in pursuing a middle path of the sort we have been describing. Today, he and his wife continue to enjoy their two wonderful sons, and life is indeed sweet. It can be sweet for you, too.

The Possibility of Possibility

There are two key antidotes to the entrapments of negative mind committee members: trustworthy allies, of which this book is one, and a manager who keeps in mind the power of *possibility*. Only possibility has the power to defeat the hopelessness Godzilla. To say it another way, hopelessness is the negation of possibility. Luckily, in the contest between them, possibility has the edge. Hopelessness trades on the past, which it depicts inaccurately. Possibility is about the future, which remains virgin and uncharted. No matter how badly Acts I and II have gone, Act III has not yet been fully scripted.

DISCOVERY 12: Acknowledging Possibility

In order to move forward, this would be a good point at which to take stock of where you, as manager,

stand on some of the issues we have been discussing. Are you now able to stop beating yourself up
over past transgressions? Do you believe in the possibility that you can wake up one day and feel (and
be) just fine? Are you willing to take a stand for these
prospects?

Some people repeatedly push the same rock up
the same hill, not believing that they will ever reach
the top. Although they have the best of intentions,
they exhaust themselves again and again, manag-
ing to lose control every time they come near the
pinnacle. Unless a doctor can show that a precise
part of your nervous system directly associated with
emotional well-being is irrevocably broken, then the
possibility of waking up fine would appear to exist,
no matter how you currently feel. So, as manager,
take stock of what the mind committee is saying
about the possibility of possibility. Notice particularly any statements issuing from the mental committee that seem to prematurely foreclose options.
Thank the committee members for any such prog-
nostications, but remind them that these are simply
opinions and predictions, not facts.

~

Possibility and Patience

Most of us are decidedly impatient. Particularly when
driven by fear and insecurity, we demand immediate outcomes. That is one of the reasons drugs and alcohol are
so popular—they change circumstances immediately. No
patience is required. But if you want to succeed in mov-

ing through the kinds of changes we are discussing, you will need to be alert to the chorus of voices that typically ruin every project by demanding instant success. People do not lose weight by dieting at a single meal—or even by "being good" for an entire week. The commitments we are discussing are for keeps! Moreover, when you find that you have eaten that extra portion of "dessert," that is not a signal to discard the entire diet plan and return to old "eating habits."

It is apt to take a year or more of working on yourself to get solid in your recovery. And then, it may take even longer to reach that wonderful plateau where you finally find yourself standing on emotionally firm ground. There will be terrific victories all along the way, as well as disturbing setbacks. However, commitment means something other than continuously checking to see which way the wind is blowing. It means keeping your word no matter what. Allow your manager's declaration for love and well-being to provide guidance about how to handle each and every circumstance, good or bad. When you transgress, clean up the resulting mess as quickly as possible. Alcohol and drugs are the short-range, high-cost solutions. We are after something less flimsy.

The Pleasures of Irresponsibility

Before we go on to the next chapter, we want to acknowledge a difficult truth: There are great rewards and pleasures to be had by acting irresponsibly and remaining comfortably ensconced in the guilty loser role. For instance, you can justify getting high a lot. You can feel sorry for yourself. If you are skillful, you can get others to feel sorry for you. You can arrange to have sex with lots of friends and strangers, even if you are married. You can eat whenever and whatever you want. You can cheat. You can slough off work when you don't feel like getting up. You can make excuses and say "screw you" to almost anyone. You don't have to take a consistent stand for anything. You can feel superior to ordinary mortals. You can give up anytime you like. Better yet, you can justify anything.

Few sane people relish all aspects of their daily lives. There's a ton of dog shit to put up with—boring, repetitive jobs, from brushing your teeth to changing diapers. If you are going to take a stance for greater responsibility and keeping your word, it might be a good idea to take an honest look at what you will be giving up in the process. This book isn't about being politically correct and simply parroting a position that plays well with a judge, spouse, boss, or friend. Perhaps, after some honest reflection, tallying up the benefits and costs, it will become clear that you do not want to live differently. Perhaps you merely wish you wanted to change. We respect that choice. There is no blame or shame attached to selecting one lifestyle over another. The universe doesn't care. In fact, being clear about where you actually are helps getting to someplace else, even if the trip gets postponed until a more propitious moment.

In the next chapter, we tackle the issue of feelings and emotions, particularly those confusing shifts in mood that get in the way of making and keeping commitments.

CHAPTER 9

Thoughts, Feelings, Actions

How many "hurtin'" country tunes do you think have been written? How many plaintive love songs? How much passionate poetry? Intense emotion seems to dominate our art, and it fuels much of the rest of our lives as well.

Simply put, humans are suckers for their feelings. When passion strikes, people seem oblivious to logic. They act for the moment. We recall a friend who was bemoaning a painful breakup of a relationship. He admitted that he had gotten overinvolved with a woman he barely knew, and he vowed that he would never let that happen again. He kept this vow—for a week. Then he met someone new. "Yeah, but this one is different," he protested, defending his latest whirlwind romance.

We lose our heads when in the grip of strong emotions. Rage, for instance, propels us into unwise, dangerous confrontations. One of our clients had been cut off by another motorist late at night on a desolate stretch of road. While the two vehicles were stopped at a traffic light, he impulsively jumped out of his car to challenge the other driver. Fortunately, the other guy sped off, avoiding a possible brawl. "What could I have been thinking?" the client said later, realizing that he had put himself in jeopardy for no particularly good reason.

Similarly, one of the authors recalls wrestling a gun away from a would-be robber. There was not a lot of cash involved, but the author, peeved at having been accosted, went on automatic pilot, risking his life over a few bucks.

Sometimes people complicate their lives by *avoiding* emotions. Drug use, we keep pointing out, is typically an emotion-mitigating strategy. Although postponing conflicts or sidestepping issues is not always harmful, chronic avoidance virtually guarantees that perfectly manageable problems will grow into headache-producing predicaments.

Knowing More About Your System

Dealing with strong feelings is easier if you understand some simple facts about how the body operates. Unfortunately, most of us are confused about the relationship between thoughts, feelings, and actions. In fact, even scientists and philosophers have had a tough time with this one.

A basic problem is that we have been taught to put thoughts, emotions, and behaviors into separate categories when, in fact, they are really just different aspects of the same thing. We do not think first, then feel, and then act. We are always thinking, feeling, and acting at virtually the same time.

Although people picture their thoughts and feelings as

being in conflict with each other or as vying for control of the system, cognitions and emotions do not compete—they cooperate. Statements such as "My head is telling me one thing, but my heart says something else" are not accurate portrayals of how the system operates.

To understand this better, you should know that thoughts are not isolated cerebral products. *Thoughts are influenced by bodily states and social situations.* Thinking is shaped by internal and external cues. Thus, the thoughts you have while visiting an ailing grandmother will be different from those you have while hitting a home run, having a romantic dinner, or being stuck in a traffic jam. Thinking about food after a big meal is different than thinking about it beforehand.

Just as thinking isn't entirely cerebral, emotion isn't entirely physical. Emotion is the word we use to describe perceived changes in bodily state. For example, at times of threat, we experience our body going into overdrive, pumping out adrenaline and priming the muscles for fight or flight. Depending on circumstances, we will label this "fear," "danger," "stress," and so on. At the other extreme, when we are feeling safe and secure, the bodily machinery shifts into low gear and we experience feeling relaxed.

Bodily postures and endocrine levels work together. The exuberance of victory and triumph calls for big, open gestures and high energy levels. After loss or defeat, we find ourselves closing up, closing down, and pulling away from others. Every activity, whether classified as cerebral or emotional, is supported by particular biological calibrations. Solving a math problem may seem like a purely mental activity, but concentration requires specific body postures and hormonal settings. Thinking burns calories just like any other of the body's activities. Therefore, to be accurate, there is no such thing as a purely mental activity. As Aldous Huxley put it, "What we think and feel and are is to a great extent determined by the state of our ductless glands and our viscera."

Playing football, making love, or doing battle all require precise physical adjustments. A fight or temper tantrum obviously involves the whole body. However, few of us realize that the same thing is true of quieter activities, such as curling up with a good book, sipping a fine wine, or admiring the sunset.

Sometimes, our physiology cannot keep pace with changing circumstances. These are the times when people report that their thoughts and feelings are pulling in opposite directions. Consider, for instance, a man who arrives home after an argument with his boss. His wife greets him at the door, expecting a warm hug and a kiss. However, he is still in the midst of his upset. The combative mood that engulfs him makes being affectionate impossible. He is primed for defense and counterattack, not for closeness and affiliation. He tells his disappointed wife that he is not in the mood. He feels bad about this, but there is not much he can do about it. The body cannot engage in two contradictory activities at once. Although people describe such clashes as being between their thoughts and their feelings, they are actually between conflicting goals—in this case, wanting to finish a fight and wanting to relax at home.

How about a situation such as the following: A man yells at himself for being a weak-willed procrastinator. His evidence: Instead of finishing his taxes, he goes out for a beer. This certainly looks like a case of emotions dominating logic. It is not. It is just the ordinary human reaction to a collision between short- and long-term goals. In such situations, we usually opt for immediate gratification over delayed, negative consequences. The beer tastes good now; the IRS will not prosecute until later. In such struggles, name-calling will not help. As we have said, guilt is a weak ally. Moreover, the situation does not indicate a lack of willpower or emotional maturity (whatever that means). What is needed is better social planning, perhaps getting a partner to help with the taxes so that the task is more social and less daunting. AA and other Twelve Step programs offer similar advice. In place of empty moralizing, AA members regularly recommend going to meetings, staying away from bars, and keeping your sponsor's phone number handy.

Furthering Detachment

Earlier we introduced the concept of detachment. We return to it now in the interest of furthering your ability to avoid becoming trapped within your personal soap opera. People who don't know better might think that there is no joy in detachment—no fun, no passion, no aliveness. Just the opposite is true. Detachment, in the Eastern sense, is not about suppressing or eliminating emotions. In fact, it calls for acknowledging and validating all of one's thoughts and bodily experiences, including those that arrive unexpectedly or which do not initially seem beneficial.

Emotions—good or bad—are not the problem. Thoughts—good or bad—are not the problem. The problem is taking thoughts and emotions too seriously. Detachment involves keeping things in perspective, letting thoughts and emotions come and go, as they will anyway. In Japan, they say that "feelings are as changeable as the Japanese sky." By this, they mean that moods and sensations come and go, shifting frequently, sometimes quickly, sometimes slowly. This lovely metaphor conveys the essence of detachment—notice, honor, enjoy (or don't enjoy) the productions of your system. Monitor the process, don't struggle against it. Even difficult feelings can be experienced as intriguing rather than exasperating. By practicing detachment, you enlarge the range of positive possibilities and eliminate much of the heaviness of your daily drama. It is not that detachment prevents upsets. It doesn't. That is what drugs are about. However, the practice of detachment renders upsets less overwhelming. They arrive in less intense form and tend to dissipate more quickly.

Remember Laura? After Laura stopped using heroin, she still was far from happy. She had to face the demons that had originally chased her into drug use. These demons had tripled in size because she had expended so much energy running from them. After being straight for about three months, Laura reported that she had been a miserable wreck all week, preoccupied with thoughts of using. Her mood of dark despair was not based on much; some random combination of cues had reawakened emotional and cognitive reactions that she thought she had long since gotten over.

Laura was asked what had stopped her from using in this situation. Her answer was instructive: "It's just like

```
STORE: 0346      REG: 03/79   TRAN#: 4103
SALE             06/30/2011   EMP:  00204
```

BORDERS

Returns

Returns of merchandise purchased from a Borders, Borders Express or Waldenbooks retail store will be permitted only if presented in saleable condition accompanied by the original sales receipt or Borders gift receipt within the time periods specified below. Returns accompanied by the original sales receipt must be made within 30 days of purchase and the purchase price will be refunded in the same form as the original purchase. Returns accompanied by the original Borders gift receipt must be made within 60 days of purchase and the purchase price will be refunded in the form of a return gift card.

Exchanges of opened audio books, music, videos, video games, software and electronics will be permitted subject to the same time periods and receipt requirements as above and can be made for the same item only.

you always say, it's just a feeling, right? And then on Saturday, it went away." It was the kind of response a therapist hopes for. The posture we call detachment smoothes out the jagged peaks and valleys of the emotional process. Laura was not feeling good, but she was beginning to learn that not feeling good did not have to be that bad. Part of the ecstasy of detachment comes from being relieved of the burden of believing that you must always do something special or immediate about upsets, losses, or cravings. Let them be, and they just might let you be.

Even when an emotion alerts you that some action may be required, the accompanying melodrama can be skipped. Great martial artists pride themselves on their ability to handle even life-and-death encounters without becoming personally attached to the outcome. They are busy on the outside, but serene within.

Why aren't human beings born "doing detachment"? Why did Eastern spiritual thinkers have to work so hard to arrive at the concept? The answer may lie in the competitive brutality of the primeval environment our ancestors faced. In those circumstances, survival was the primary and all-consuming objective. Without survival, there would have been no point in discussing detachment. Rapidly mobilizing for fight or flight was a high priority. Though the environment most of us confront these days is more civilized, our biological and cultural systems continue to reflect that primitive tooth-and-claw mentality. In terms of today's world, our systems are set incorrectly. We have too much of what was once a good thing. We need the kind of fine-tuning that thoughtful reflection can provide. And, in the words of the English poet and critic Samuel Taylor Coleridge, reflection is the one art "of which man should be master." The next chapter is about practical methods for mastering detachment and deepening our reflective powers.

CHAPTER 10

Practicing Detachment

Detachment involves allowing yourself to simply experience whatever you are feeling and thinking. You do not overidentify with it. You do not consider any of it permanent. You come to realize that life never gets so good that it cannot be bad again, nor does it ever get so bad that it cannot be good again. Detachment means, in effect, permitting thoughts and feelings to make themselves known and pass through the system. Thoughts and reactions convey information about how your system is functioning at any given moment. They do not always require an immediate decision, a definite conclusion, or a dramatic action. Detachment does not interfere with accomplishing necessary tasks. It prevents going into overdrive and galloping off unproductively in too many directions. It does not imply being impassive, colorless, or disinterested. Detachment is arguably the core tool your manager needs to propel you along the path to a drug-free existence.

DISCOVERY 13: An Inch That's Greater Than a Mile

The goal of this exercise is to teach you how to have emotional reactions without letting them have you. Mr. or Ms. Manager, the idea is for you to learn to stand your ground in the face of the emotional bullies. For the first step, prepare to place your hand over your face—literally. Now, have your hand cover your entire face and, as best you can, clench it. Keep it there for the count of three and then come back to this page.

The sensation your hand produced is analogous to the grip of strong emotional states and persistent thoughts. They blind you as a whole, destroying perspective and foreclosing options. The system goes into emergency action, with no time for you as a compassionate manager to reflect on circumstances and explore possibilities. In the midst of upset, your ability to govern is greatly reduced.

Now, try placing that same hand directly over your face. However, this time, take it away immediately and quickly place it behind your head. This is analogous to running away from upsetting emotions. The ways to run are numerous, as we keep mentioning. Note that either strategy—running with or running away from—involves a loss of perspective. The mind banditos get to dominate.

Once again, put your hand over your face. However, this time, position your hand so that it is about an inch in front of your face. Keep it there to the count of, let's say, ten. This is analogous to detachment. The upset is still in front of you, but the space you created between it and you allows you to use it rather than letting it use you. You are *facing* the upset but are not being enslaved by it. Although the upset is definitely in your field of vision, you are no longer blinded by it. Allowing it to be an inch from your face, you are still frightened, angry, sad, or confused. But you have also added an ounce of "so what" to the emotional recipe.

With that inch of detachment in place, you are still not a happy camper. You may continue to shake and quake. But that little wiggle room transforms the experience. This is what Laura described when discussing the kind of misery that in the past would have propelled her toward heroin. Her emerging ability to see her feelings for what they were—just feelings—made all the difference.

∼

As you make a habit of facing rather than fleeing or over-reacting to your inner bullies, the effect gathers momentum. Detachment generates an ever-widening creative field. Allowing is the key to detachment. To quote British psychiatrist Claire Weekes, you *float* rather than *fight* (1976, p. 33). Authors Alan Marlatt and Judith Gordon, in their book on relapse prevention (1985, p. 64), suggest the image of surfing as a useful metaphor. By surfing the waves of thought and emotion, you ride them safely back to shore and allow them to ebb away of their own accord.

David's Bugs

David, one of the authors, is phobic when it comes to certain insects. He also has an aversion to horror movies. A while ago, he was watching a television show that dealt with the issue of whether irradiated ants could ever evolve into giants. (Fortunately, the answer is no.)

The show was more theatrical than scientific, and the ants, shown in close-up, were portrayed as if they had already become giants. David's reaction to this wasn't helped by his having just read a newspaper article about the threat of deadly fire ants migrating north from South America. The article pointed out that these ants had evolved to the point where they were now able to thrive in colder climates. The author of the article graphically depicted the ants' ability to swarm and sting vulnerable individuals to death.

Of course, David imagined himself the victim of just such an attack. It was not that David chose to think these thoughts—they thought David! The article further stated that biologists were bringing in a parasitic micro-insect species to infect the fire ants, literally eating their heads off from the inside. As far as David was concerned, that added tidbit of information, intended to be reassuring, only served to escalate the "yuck factor" of the experience.

Sitting in front of the TV and watching the show about ants, David felt a familiar surge of apprehension. What should he do? Turn off the TV? Change the channel? Especially given that he was working on this book, he felt obliged to cope with the challenge the way we are advising here.

With his manager in place, he was able to create that necessary first inch of detachment. He listened with interest (as well as dread) to his internal conversation. Some committee members demanded immediate escape, but the manager and his allies urged staying tuned in. One annoying internal voice reminded David of how badly he had reacted, as a kid, to seeing the 3-D version of the classic Vincent Price horror film *House of Wax*. It led to nights of having to sleep with the lights on.

There were devious mind demons who argued, "What's the big deal anyway—who's gonna know if you turn it off?" And, then, there was the usual "you're just a loser, after all" gang, always looking for an opportunity to stir up trouble. As usual, physical sensations intermingled with this mind stuff, resulting in creepy, crawly, cold, and clammy feelings, as well as a pounding heart and a sense of growing exhaustion. A full-fledged phobic response had been launched.

However, David's manager stood his ground. He left the remote control on the table and committed himself to observing—but not fighting—his reactions to the program. With the inch of detachment generated by that stance, he actually found himself enjoying portions of the presentation. Hey, it was interesting stuff! Of course, he had to be willing to face those giant bugs coming to eat his brains out, if it came to that. He wasn't going anywhere, no matter what. He would allow his thoughts, feelings, and images to freely come and go. With that bedrock commitment in place, the emotional storm subsided.

Good Self-Talk

That first inch of detachment can be cemented in place by having your manager rehearse basic, trustworthy declarations that derive from your commitments. In an impending storm, good self-talk matters. Phrases like "I can and will stay on track, no matter what" can keep the mind demons at bay.

What makes good self-talk effective is practicing it while certain mind demons are flexing their muscles. At first, it may seem like an uphill battle to say positive things to yourself while you are not feeling good. However, as they say in AA, "Fake it till you make it." To take a stand for something different and liberating, your manager has to keep speaking the truth *however you happen to be feeling*. Otherwise, he or she inadvertently cooperates in your enslavement. When feeling under attack, your manager reaffirms basic commitments as often as necessary, and for as long as it takes. Of course, the manager is respectful and thanks members of the mind committee for their opinions. At the same time, he or she reminds the committee members of the larger mission. Don't worry about your manager sounding repetitious. Repetition is good because it literally and figuratively helps create new and useful neural pathways. Besides, initially, all we care about is generating that first crucial inch of detachment.

Hacking a New Path

Biologically speaking, the neural pathways in your brain associated with serious upsets are wide and deep, having been trod for so long and with such intensity. By now they are veritable boulevards. It will take some time to hack a new path, or to clear an old, underused byway to cheerier terrain. Stay with it and it becomes easier. Anytime the guilty mind demons grab the microphone, have your manager repeat that even if their accusations are true (at least according to Mode No. 1 logic), you still deserve a life of love, compassion, and well-being (from the perspective of Mode No. 2). Moreover, this stand for self-compassion implies compassion for others—*with absolutely no one excluded.* You see, you cannot save yourself without doing the same for everyone else. Life can be lovely in its symmetry. With each repetition of this basic and powerful message, your manager will gain a better footing.

Jack's Story

Jack came into the office of one of the authors with a serious cocaine and alcohol problem. He was in his mid-thirties and had, several years before, owned his own home and run a successful business. He and his wife had four young children. When he came for help he was broke, having lost his home, his business, and his family. It would take Jack a year to reconcile with his wife and another year for him to land a meaningful job.

Jack had become a workaholic by the time he was in his teens, and he had turned to drugs to give him the boost he needed to keep going. Alcohol was his way of mellowing out. Once he stopped using, Jack began to notice that he suffered severe panic attacks—"waking nightmares," he called them. One of the strategies that helped Jack was good self-talk, which he labeled "rationalizing." Of course, the term rationalization usually carries negative connotations. However, for Jack it meant reinforcing his primary goals and commitments through self-discussion.

After treatment, Jack complained that he still needed to "rationalize" when conditions got stressful. He worried that his continued reliance on such self-talk meant that he wasn't completely out of the woods—that he was still sick or deficient in some way. Of course, this was a perpetuation of the kind of fear messages his negative mind demons loved to spout. Jack needed to know that even those of us who lead rich and fulfilling lives continue to use self-talk to provide a personal rudder. Being okay doesn't mean never having moments of confusion or pangs of regret.

A powerful CEO with a reputation for self-confidence was once asked if he didn't have some personal doubts from time to time, perhaps late at night, when everyone else had gone to bed. His answer was surprising. He chuckled and said that he surely didn't have to wait until the middle of the night to be visited by the gremlins of uncertainty. Doubt and hesitancy were familiar companions. However, he had established a good working relationship with them—he let them be and they let him be. He knew he would always have doubts but was under no obligation to let them rock the boat.

DISCOVERY 14: Practicing Self-Talk

Invent some good self-talk. Come up with a list of five statements that seem really solid and nourishing. By the way, you do not have to believe them to be true. However, they have to be the kinds of state-ments which, if true, would move you toward fuller self-expression and compassionate love for yourself and others. Here are some examples from other people's lists: "I can handle whatever happens," "I am worthwhile," "I deserve good things," "I am in charge of myself," "I am significant," "I intend to be happy," "I have the right to love others, regardless of whether those sentiments are reciprocated," "I have the right to take care of myself," and "I am not here to prove anything."

Now, Mr. or Ms. Manager, picture a time when everything seemed to be falling apart and the mind demons were yelling especially loudly—perhaps yesterday. Take control of the microphone and re-hearse your list of five solid self-statements. If the mind demons are still protesting, run through the list a second or third time. By the way, be sure to let the demons have their say. Assure them that their message has been heard, and then continue with your list.

Observe your reactions to this exercise. Did the degree to which your self-statements seemed right and logical increase or decrease during the exer-cise? As with everything new and challenging in this book, patience and practice are crucial for success.

∼

In the next chapter we say more about dealing with the grip of negative beliefs and the role of commitment. The chapter begins with the story of another one of our clients—Fred.

CHAPTER 11

Strengthening Commitment

Fred sought counseling for an alcohol problem. His story, although especially intense, is only one of dozens that could be told to illustrate how powerful commitments help individuals stay on track, even in the face of calamitous circumstances. Danger and hardship make keeping one's word more challenging. However, it is also during adverse times that steadfast commitments prove their worth.

Fred's father had been a violent drunk who beat up his wife and terrorized Fred and his two older brothers while they were growing up. Fred was the baby of the family and was thus protected more than the others by his mom. Life at home became increasingly terrifying until, when Fred was about fifteen, his father died suddenly of a heart attack. Fred experienced the event with a peculiar mixture of relief and sadness.

Throughout school, Fred relied on alcohol to calm his nerves. Fortunately, his substance use did not prevent him from becoming a successful and responsible professional. It did, however, become increasingly troublesome later in life following a series of difficult life stresses. First, Fred's beloved mother became ill and eventually died in a delusional state. At about the same time, his first marriage ended. Fred later remarried and his second wife gave birth shortly after their marriage. Sadly, however, their daughter died in infancy. Fred rolled with the punches in his usual quiet, levelheaded way, but the more his losses mounted, the more he drank.

Then Fred's oldest brother murdered his wife and killed himself in a murder-suicide that stunned the community. To add to the family's troubles, Fred's wife was diagnosed with a severe chronic illness. They had four young children by then, and Fred had to stop working in order to help care for them. As if this wasn't enough, Fred also discovered that his other brother had embezzled the funds their father had left for the grandchildren, Fred's children. Fred reluctantly reported the theft to the police. His only respite at the end of the day seemed to be the bottle. And, really, who could blame Fred for feeling like a perpetual loser? Like Job, Fred pressed on, only to be hit in the gut over and over again.

Fred was a thoughtful man. He could see that no amount of complaining would alter the tragedies the family endured. He recognized that the only way to move forward was to risk yet another roll of the dice. Fred's mind demons worked overtime issuing anger and fear messages. However, their noisy pronouncements could not shake Fred's basic commitment to his family's survival. His wife and family needed him to be strong and persevering, and after thinking hard and long about the matter, he realized that what he most wanted in life was to be there for them. He had an intuitive sense that his own level of self-satisfaction hinged on the welfare of the family unit. He made a conscious decision to dedicate himself anew to the prosperity of his wife and children. Having made that pledge to himself, he reassured his wife that he was there for the long haul. He gave up alcohol altogether and accepted a job with flexible hours so that he could accommodate his wife's changing state of health. He took stock of his blessings—which, he discovered, were considerable. He was healthy and had a loving wife, adorable kids, a respectable job, some money in the bank, and a comfortable place to live. He and his wife worked out ways to enjoy their children and have fun together. They weren't sure what challenges the future would bring, but they knew the smart money was on sticking together and making each day count. The legal proceedings against his brother continued, but Fred was convinced that reporting his brother's transgression to the authorities was the right thing to do. He believed that it would ultimately bring the family closer together.

Obviously, taking a firm stand for compassion does not mean magically solving all of one's problems. Fred still had good days and bad. There continued to be difficult choices to be made, for example, about which treatments his wife should undertake and when. However, even in his darkest moments, Fred kept in mind the guiding premise of his commitment. Whenever he was unsure what to do, he attempted to calculate which option would most enhance his family's ability to remain intact and maximize its level of well-being and satisfaction. He knew that feelings were temporary. When you do the right thing for the right reason, emotions that once raised havoc tend to fade in significance. Commitment is the anchor that makes it possible to weather life's daily buffeting.

The Hoax of Winning

Most of us are entirely too preoccupied with the drama of winning and losing. We would be wise to cultivate some of the serenity that characterized legendary martial artists. By fully accepting the nature of the contest (and all of its possible consequences), they were able to maintain their detachment even during the heat of battle. They had already won, just by being able to participate. Therefore, they could devote themselves to playing the game at hand, rather than constantly worrying about the score. The Zen saying, "win first, then play" captures this useful and freeing perspective.

If we weren't so caught up in winning, we would see immediately that—in the final analysis—there are no real wins. In life, we ultimately have to give up whatever we have managed to amass. At the end of the day, win or lose, we are obliged to yield the field to the next group of players. That is the natural progression. Trophies inevitably sit on a shelf and get dusty. In the game of life, the game counts more than the prizes. The stance we recommend—exemplified by Fred's strong commitment to himself and his family—is to play hard, honor your agreements, remain perpetually curious about the next inning, and remind yourself, from time to time, that it's all just a game.

Of course, the way to really lose is to entertain the delusion that you can ever really win. By definition, truly satisfying games must involve a mix of wins and losses. If, for instance, you were to consistently win at Ping-Pong, you would have to change the rules or stiffen the competition. Otherwise, boredom would set in. Many people have the false belief that the allure of gambling is the possibility of the big win. Erving Goffman, the well-known sociologist, claims otherwise. He suggests that the excitement has much more to do with the risk of losing. A constant series of wins—even big wins—becomes tedious.

We had a friend who had a system for winning at blackjack. He visited the casinos, betting small amounts to avoid attracting attention and quitting when he had made a small profit. He did this several times a week, varying which casinos he frequented. We ran into this gentleman after he had been pursuing his method for several months. We asked how it was going. He said he was no longer using his system. "You mean it didn't work?" we said. "No, it worked perfectly," he replied, "but it wasn't any fun—it wasn't gambling." He explained that working his system took time and concentration. It was exactly like having a regular job, which is what he had been hoping to avoid in the first place.

Some people become obsessed with the idea of winning. They want to win even if they no longer enjoy playing and have no real interest in the prizes. Some would sooner withdraw from the competition than risk coming in second. For instance, a client of ours gave up the game of tennis entirely as soon as he realized that he could not take first place in the city championships. Like a child having a tantrum, he stalked off the court in a fit of self-disgust.

Perhaps this kind of heavy investment in being on top harks back to the days when the human species faced an environment of relentless scarcity and danger. Even prosperous tribes had to be concerned about an instant reversal of fortunes, including crop failures, warring neighbors, and unpredictably harsh winters. The human mind tends to overreact to potential threat. We always want to win, to be right, and to be in control. We hate losing, being wrong, or feeling dominated. Evidently we did not rise to the top of the food chain by being an easy-going species!

Many of us run when we aren't being chased. We criticize ourselves before we can be disparaged by anyone else. The mind's logic seems to be: "You can't really attack me on a point I have already conceded." Also, once the mind becomes obsessed with proving its own worth, past fame and fortune are rarely enough. "Yes," certain mind banditos say smugly, "you won *that* promotion, but perhaps it was a fluke." "You fooled them up until now, but they will soon find out that you are a fraud." Trying to quell such doubts by reciting past victories is like using a flashlight to illuminate a black hole. The beam of past accomplishments is never bright enough to penetrate the expanse of potential gloom. Any minor gaffe or sign of disapproval can trigger a fresh torrent of anxious ruminations.

Enduring tranquility comes only through the recognition that self-worth does not hinge on external awards and accomplishments. In truth, you are not required to defend or justify who you are. You are already perfectly whole, complete, and sufficient—no defense is necessary. Being born was the big win (and the big loss).

Anything you achieve thereafter is extra, just icing on the cake.

Throughout life, you always have the choice of operating from a context of sufficiency or deficiency. A sufficient person is okay as is. However, if you operate from the context of deficiency, you sentence yourself to a never-ending improvement battle. No matter how hard you try, you can never improve enough to satisfy those internal banditos. Even if you get better, it is never better enough! The alternative, the one we recommend, is to give up the improvement game altogether and declare yourself sufficient from the outset. Then, enjoy and appreciate each accomplishment as it comes along, not as a proof of worth, but as the next installment of your continuing saga. From the perspective of the middle way, no matter what you achieve, you will still be nothing—and everything. Important and unimportant, serious and trivial. An Iranian client shared that, in his native country, they have a proverb that, loosely translated, says, "When one gets too serious, visit a graveyard."

Taking the Good with the Bad

The First Noble Truth of Buddhism is that life is imbued with suffering. Pain and pleasure are paired phenomena: There is no rose without a thorn. In terms of conventional Mode No. 1 logic, we welcome happiness and defend against distress. We celebrate wins and mourn losses. However, at a higher level (Mode No. 2), it is apparent that happiness and sorrow are linked. Successes and failures are mutually self-defining. The middle way, in which everything is accepted for what it is, allows what Buddhists call *Tathata*, a deep wisdom that leads to the experience of peace, balance, and inner stillness. The related term *Tathagata* is another name for Buddha, one with such great wisdom that she or he knows and accepts just what is so; nothing more, nothing less.

Remember that when the mind banditos emphasize the negative, they think they are being your friends. They are working to insure your physical and psychological survival, attempting to fulfill their mandate. However, they typically go overboard. They are attuned to danger but blind to the costs of defensiveness. They have no capacity to notice that every life game—climbing mountains, playing football, speaking up at a meeting, venturing into a relationship—entails risk. Without risk, there can be no participation. Without participation, there can be no joy or satisfaction. Only your manager, operating on the basis of a firm and broad commitment, can balance exposure and opportunity. In doing so, your manager should keep in mind the following basic truths: Life will be over soon enough. Given the vastness of space and time, your individual existence will soon be forgotten. Playing hard is more fun than lazing around. Establishing and keeping commitments makes life meaningful. Even if you manage to accomplish more in your lifetime than any other human being who ever lived, it will all still be just a game.

The next discovery exercise is about further strengthening commitment.

DISCOVERY 15: Attack of the Aliens

Imagine that aliens have abducted you. They want to perform some brainwashing experiments. They have begun by trying to convince you that $1 + 1 = 3$. If they can get you to accept that "truth," they will conclude that humans are easily influenced and that taking over the planet will be pretty easy. So they have put you in a box, and every day, in different ways, they hammer away at the notion.

You hold out for a very long time, but eventually the aliens convince you that $1 + 1$ really does equal 3. Furthermore, they set it up so that whenever this new "insight" is challenged, you react with upset and confusion. In our terminology, you have become attached to your new belief system.

Your attachment (and your attachment to that attachment) would be fierce. If anyone argued against it you would feel upset, threatened, and confused. Take a few minutes to imagine the reality of such a situation.

If this seems like too much of a stretch, note that if and when you feel compelled to get high, you are able to convince yourself—despite all of your past experience—that this time it will be different. In other words, you base your willingness to get high on a powerful attachment that might strike objective observers as shortsighted and illogical—the results of a specialized form of brainwashing.

In any event, once you have acquired the dogma that $1 + 1 = 3$ (or any other new belief) a special mind committee member is assigned the duty of defending that piece of information. The mind demon is able to mobilize powerful physical sensations to reinforce its outlook. If and when you are rescued from the aliens, that mind demon would resist deprogramming attempts, no matter how well-meaning. In fact, the mind demon in charge of $1 + 1 = 3$ will certainly attempt to convince you that all deprogrammers are your enemies.

Take some more time now and imagine what we have just described within the context of your drug and alcohol cravings. At the same time, see if there is a fundamental logical principle that can protect you from any such alien sneak attacks. Can we equip your manager with a truth so basic and solid that it cannot be dislodged or superseded despite changes in mood, shifts in circumstances, or fancy brainwashing techniques? We need something your manager can use to withstand the pressures of any $1 + 1 = 3$ invasion. If we can find such a truth, it is the tool to use to sustain detachment in the face of emotionally provocative or intense experiences. Perhaps a truth you will find useful is that, just as $1 + 1 = 2$, you are a perfect part of the universal whole. You may not be able to control what others think and do; however, under all circumstances, you can affirm your unconditional commitment to express love and contribute to the well-being of the species.

∼

In the next chapter, we argue that most of daily life consists of a series of dramatic enactments. We are the producers and stars of these playlets. If we take our soap operas too seriously, we can become prisoners of out-moded and unproductive scripts. On the other hand, the recognition that so much of life is just play-acting yields a new sense of mastery and control over our existence.

CHAPTER 12

Life as Theater

Shakespeare was right. All the world is a stage. Our lives are dramatic productions in which we simultaneously serve as playwrights, actors, audience members, and critics. Relatives, bosses, co-workers, and friends are extras sent over from central casting. Of course, they perceive the situation the other way around—they believe that *they* are the stars and that *we* are members of the supporting cast.

Human beings create and convey meaning through the stories they enact. That is why mathematician and philosopher James P. Carse argues that if we "cannot tell a story about what happened to us, nothing has happened to us" (1986, p. 167). The tales we exchange and the roles we play shape who we are and what we become.

Without such narratives, we would be like aimless wanderers, moving through each day's events without any larger sense of purpose. If we were deprived of our stories, we would have to spend our days responding only to immediate needs—eating when hungry, drinking when thirsty, and sleeping when tired. We would have no reason (or ability) to reminisce about the past or plan for the future. It is our storytelling skills that transform everyday existence into something more memorable (and potentially more troublesome) than the gratification of momentary urges.

To appreciate how life might look if we lost our ability to create and participate in stories, consider the film *Groundhog Day*. As you may recall, Bill Murray's character keeps waking up at the beginning of the very same day. Life refuses to move forward. He is caught in a repeating loop. Tragically, something of this sort actually happens to individuals suffering from certain types of neurological damage. Having lost their ability to track events, they keep asking to be introduced to the very same people and they are forced to repeatedly check to see if they finished tying their shoelaces. Their information-processing deficits keep them stuck in the present. They have lost the ability to add new chapters to their life story.

As we have said, our personal dramas make life meaningful. Moreover, every good tale involves movement from point A to point B. People can put up with enormous frustrations provided their lives seem to be going somewhere. It is when personal narratives break down, as in the Groundhog Day scenario, that depression sets in. When things are going poorly, people need to see some light at the end of the tunnel. They have difficulty tolerating the notion that Act II is just going to be a repeat of Act I.

Fortunately, scripts can always be rewritten. The second act need never parallel the first. As personality theorist George Kelly used to say, "There is nothing so obvious that its appearance is not altered when it is seen in a different light" (1969, p. 227). Even when external conditions stay much the same, we can always change what we do with them. As Marcel Proust put it, "The only real voyage of discovery consists not in seeking new landscapes but in having new eyes."

Larry was a successful writer with alcohol problems. He had grown up with a father who was routinely abusive. Perhaps for that reason, many of Larry's core beliefs concerned the untrustworthiness of others. He believed he was cursed with bad karma, that the forces of life were stacked against him. Based on his childhood experiences, Larry had put together a dismal life script that he perpetuated for many years.

Larry made great strides in counseling. In rapid succession, he gave up alcohol, marijuana, and cigarettes. Just as important, he was willing to abandon the gloomy script he had constructed for himself, realizing that his sullen demeanor mainly succeeded in driving others away. He began to see that not every pessimistic thought had to be aired. Under certain conditions, silence is golden.

In addition, at the therapist's suggestion, he stopped publicly bad-mouthing his wife. He nevertheless continued to consider her a critical and uncaring woman. In therapy, Larry admitted that when they first met he had found her negativity appealing. He mistook her acerbic style as evidence that they were soul mates and, frankly, more upbeat women made him edgy. However, over the years, he became increasingly impatient with her constant complaining. At least in theory, Larry knows that genuine compassion for oneself means nurturing one's compassion for others—even if, as in his wife's case, they seem initially unresponsive and impossible to reach.

Larry had more immediate success rethinking his views about his childhood. He saw that being whole and complete means acknowledging that the entirety of your past—the bad as well as the good—contributes to who you are. For example, had it not been for his father's abuse, Larry probably would have become a logger like his dad, rather than the writer he now likes being. Larry could see how he could even draw inspiration from the assaults he had weathered, and how, as a writer, he could make good use of all those elements in his background. Although he still would not have wished some of his past experiences on his worst enemy, he began to consider them a unique resource and valuable personal legacy. No longer did he wish that his memories of those days could be wiped clean. Like the proverbial alchemist who changes base metals into gold, Larry found new ways to turn his past suffering into a creative treasure chest.

Larry's story illustrates that circumstances do not, in and of themselves, fix present reactions or dictate future prospects. Being fired from a job can be a humbling failure or a freeing opportunity. A divorce can signal the collapse of a family or the first phase of a healthy personal reappraisal. Nothing is all good or all bad. We had a colleague who worked for many years with the homeless. He always cautioned the rest of us against forming stereotypical judgments about their situation. He pointed out, for instance, that some street people have hefty bank accounts—not all homeless individuals are destitute. Some have repeatedly rebuffed family offers of shelter and assistance. For various reasons, there are a few who have avoided collecting family inheritances. A substantial minority take pride in their nontraditional life style and steadfastly reject any attempts to induct them into mainstream society. This is even true in cities like Philadelphia, where winters can be harsh and summers can be oppressive.

At the other end of the socioeconomic spectrum, many people with well-paying, high-visibility jobs are not content. For instance, Marlene, a thirty-something woman, sought counseling because of a cocaine problem. She was a successful vice-president of an influential media firm. She had a devoted, loving husband. As they say, she had it all. But for Marlene, having it all was not enough. She was a workaholic who used cocaine to help get through her seventy-hour work week. She had taken virtually no time off in years. She felt driven and, in her eyes, her many past accomplishments amounted to very little.

As a child, Marlene was dyslexic. Schooled in a rural area of Manitoba, she dreaded being called on in class. Her mother was a feminist who always preached that women should be able to fend for themselves because, she said, "You can never count on a man!" Her other message was that females needed to be at least twice as good as males if they were going to succeed.

When she finished college, Marlene was determined to prove that she could make it. Of course, behind the need to prove something is usually the nagging suspicion that it isn't true. Marlene struggled relentlessly to show that she was better, smarter, and more industrious than everyone else. In counseling, it finally dawned on her that her competitive striving was inherently unsatisfying. The feeling of approval she sought eluded her. She felt lonely and insecure at work, and her frantic schedule had begun to take its toll on her marriage. Marlene realized that she was sort of sleepwalking through a life that conformed more to her mother's goals than her own. By default, she was quickly moving beyond the point where she could expect to have children of her own and raise a family.

For Marlene, it was not too late to reevaluate her objectives. As the saying goes, the problem with the path you are on is that you are very apt to get to where you are going! From a middle way perspective, people are always entitled to tweak the script and introduce new plot twists. The shame is that so few recognize their options. They remain asleep up to their retirement years and beyond—perpetuating, through force of habit, life games that are no longer joyful, and continuing to collect trophies that have long since lost their meaning.

The range of plots people can enact is virtually limitless. Thus, it is surprising that people so often stick to a few repetitive, tiresome, costly scenarios. Before counseling, for example, Larry would trot out his stock script of complaints on practically every occasion. In addition to railing against his wife, he called his editor stupid, his relatives selfish, his friends fickle, and his children unappreciative.

Of course, at a basic level, the role of complainer always works. The individual can portray himself or herself as the victim of an unjust world. The rewards of this lifestyle include self-righteousness and sympathy. Unfortunately, what is sacrificed is love, satisfaction, and a sense of mastery.

Drew had been smoking up to ten marijuana joints a day since he was a teen. He was essentially friendless and frequently out of work. He persuaded himself that men were boring and women were devious. Therefore, neither group was worth spending time with. Even at Narcotics Anonymous meetings, Drew felt disaffected. His counselor pointed out that his generalizations about people certainly painted him into a lonely corner. Drew retorted defensively that it wasn't his fault that people sucked. He was simply telling it like it is.

What finally helped Drew shift to a different place, psychologically, was a form of fixed role therapy. This is a clever treatment strategy invented by George Kelly in the fifties. It involves a special kind of play-acting. Drew was to pretend that he had gone on vacation. While he was away, an alter ego named Robert, Drew's middle name, would take over for him. To avoid confusing others, Robert would still respond to the name Drew, although he would be thinking of himself as being someone else. Drew and the counselor worked out a role for Robert that involved a change in perspective. Unlike Drew, Robert usually gave people the benefit of the doubt—he rarely made snap judgments. He was genuinely interested in learning about the details of people's attitudes—how they thought about the world and each other. Whenever possible, he would ask people questions and listen carefully to the answers. After a couple of weeks, Drew was brought back from vacation to discuss and interpret his alter ego's experiences.

In the fixed role approach, it is never assumed that the alter ego's assumptions will become a permanent part of the individual's role or personality. The exercise is presented as a time-limited experiment. The purpose is to be able to gather data about how the world looks when you put on a different set of glasses. People playing a fixed role do not necessarily change their outward behavior that much. However, if the exercise goes well, they give themselves an opportunity to try on an alternative perspective.

George Kelly used exercises like fixed role therapy to remind people that their perceptions were colored by their suppositions and that there was no reason for them to slavishly adhere to yesterday's scripts. They could keep reinventing themselves. He frequently told a cautionary tale about a dean at a well-known midwestern university. The gentlemen's resume indicated that he had twenty years of experience in college administration. "Not so," argued one of his detractors, "he has had just *one* year of experience, repeated twenty times."

We call another costly script that many adopt "living in the hypothetical." The main theme in such scenarios is that "life would be great if . . ." or "I will be happy when. . . ." Individuals who follow this script can be considered "this-isn't-it-aholics." They do not seem to notice that even the grandest goals lose importance once they have been achieved. The construction of the human mind insures that past victories will fade in significance. Few of us, for instance, continue celebrating our high school graduations year in and year out. Similarly, Bill Gates has probably gotten over the excitement of being the world's richest man.

Life is a motion picture, not a static canvas. Our attention inevitably shifts from past accomplishments to current problems and future challenges. As soon as we solve one problem, a hundred more problems show up to take its place. There is always someone new to meet, something new to covet, something new to fret about. In a way, this is fortunate. If we dwelled on past glories, life would come to a grinding halt as soon as we bought that new car we dreamt about or finally received the promotion we were anticipating. By definition, wants and desires are always about that which hasn't yet happened. There is no point in waiting for some momentous occasion to make you happy. A better strategy, as the title of a Ram Dass book by the same name suggests, is to "be here now," finding satisfaction in each day's adventures (1971). In fact, satisfaction can only be experienced now. As they say in AA, life needs to be taken "one day at a time." In the next chapter, we talk more about personal scripts and how they can be repaired, revised, and rejuvenated.

CHAPTER 13

Revising the Script

As we indicated in the previous chapter, it is easier to revise personal stories if you understand that they are just stories. Life options are not written in stone. For instance, even if you were abused in childhood, you can—today—behave any way you like. Part of what has made our species so successful is our ability to break through even impossible-seeming barriers. Of course, the victim role has its advantages. For one thing, if you think of yourself as damaged goods you have a built-in excuse for almost anything that happens. However, there are also advantages to abandoning roles such as the injured party or weary warrior. In fact, there is some evidence that adopting a more open and trusting approach to relationships forestalls further abuse. For some reason, victims and perpetrators tend to be drawn to one another. Paradoxically, the stance of guardedness and fragility that many abused individuals adopt may attract the very low-life types they hope to avoid—a perfect example of the Zen principle that "whatever you resist, persists."

We realize that habitual roles and customs can be difficult to shuck. Hindus, for example, consider cows sacred animals. They find it exceedingly difficult to think of beef as food, even when faced with starvation. Yet, at root, the sanctity of the cow is simply part of a belief system, not a fixed aspect of objective reality. Therefore, it is always possible for a Hindu individual to learn to eat and enjoy beef. We have no desire to talk vegetarians into being carnivorous. However, we think it is essential for all of us to keep in mind that even deep-seated, culturally sanctioned beliefs are, in principle, modifiable. They are just opinions, judgments, decisions, stories, scripts—products of our systems at work. Individual viewpoints are similarly malleable.

One of the authors works with severely phobic individuals. His clinical experience confirms what the research suggests—that even the most rigidly fearful individuals can successfully challenge their avoidant behavior. Breaking one's own rules can feel like an arduous, risky process, but success is always possible. When fearful individuals emerge on the other side of their phobias, they often wonder what all the fuss was about. For instance, a woman who was terrified of flying finally got on an airplane in order to be at the bedside of her critically ill daughter. In retrospect, she regretted how long she had allowed her fear of flying to run her life and limit her mobility. A client who was initially unwilling to ingest medication broke through his phobic fear when a life-threatening infection forced him to take antibiotics. Prior to that, he had steadfastly refused even over-the-counter preparations, even though this meant putting up with excruciating dental pain, the agonies of the flu, and so on. After his successful experience with antibiotics, he reversed engines and started to demand antibiotics whenever he got sick. His physician had to remind him that not every ailment requires a prescription and that overusing antibiotics can be as dangerous as avoiding them altogether.

In these examples, people changed their behavior under dramatic circumstances. However, script revisions can occur at any time. Years ago, one of the authors was involved in an experiment on pain tolerance. Subjects were challenged to keep their hands in circulating ice water, kept just above the freezing point. At first, neither the author nor any of the other project staff were able to keep their hands immersed in the water for more than fifteen or twenty seconds. Subjects rarely lasted as long as a minute, even when they were offered money and other incentives to keep going. Everyone involved believed that the physical sensations became unbearable after a short time.

One day, however, the staff watched a subject keep his hand in the water for the full five minutes that the safety limit allowed. After watching him perform this feat, one of the assistants was inspired to equal the subject's performance. He reasoned that if the subject could do it, so could he. In short order, everyone associated with the project was easily reaching the five-minute time limit. They just needed to see that it could be done.

It is a bit like what happened in 1954 when Roger Bannister ran the mile in less than four minutes—previously considered a physical impossibility. Soon after, a succession of people equaled or surpassed his record. By 1957, sixteen runners had broken through the fabled barrier. Why? Many argue that it was because Bannister showed that it was a myth.

Sure, keeping your hand in ice water is uncomfortable. However, once you make up your mind to do it, the task is far less daunting than it originally seemed. Just as it was for phobic clients who later surmounted their fears, the constraints are mostly in the stories we tell ourselves. Project members were convinced that they knew their limits. As it turned out, they were misled by their beliefs.

The Power of Commitment

We have said that the prerequisite to being able to crawl out of a restrictive personal narrative is the realization that it is just a story—a set of assumptions, a role description, a plot line. However, certain yarns of ours become fixed dogmas. Changing these usually requires a clear commitment to an important goal. The clarity of the commitment gives the person the courage to abandon a familiar narrative and venture into relatively uncharted territory. As Seneca, the famous Roman orator, said, "Our plans miscarry because they have no aim. When a man does not know what harbor he is making for, no wind is the right wind."

An emboldening commitment—for instance, dedicating your life to compassion, adventure, and self-expression—provides the vision needed to choose among alternatives in difficult situations. What should you do if you get high again tonight? What should you do if the court issues a restraining order? What should you do if you are diagnosed with cancer? Only a broad-based commitment can provide the guidance the mind manager needs to navigate life's exigencies.

By the way, although we are sticklers about the advisability of honoring your commitments, we caution against making a big deal about it. Your manager can keep a steady hand on the wheel without becoming melodramatic or engaging in grand gestures. Being ultra-serious about life just wastes energy and makes you look foolish. A lighter perspective works better and is less apt to get you in trouble. We agree with Fran Leibowitz that it often helps to remember that "life is just something to do when you can't get to sleep."

DISCOVERY 16: Reflecting on Your Life as a Story

Now, let's explore the notion of you as personal playwright. Imagine yourself waking up in an episode of *The Twilight Zone*. In this episode, you find yourself sitting in a movie theater watching your life story unfold on the screen. The story begins with a kind of prequel showing your parents together before you were born. It then takes you on a journey from your birth until now.

Gaze at the screen in your mind's eye and begin to watch your life unfold. First, you will want to get an image of being born. Who was around at the time? What were their reactions? Next, move on to your preschool years, perhaps focusing on a couple of specific incidents, such as being left alone in your crib, visiting a relative, or having a birthday party.

Where were you living at the time? Who was in your household? What was the theme of those early years?

Now, imagine a few scenes from your school years. What surprises occurred? Which people were important to you? Did you have a best friend? Whom did you despise or resent? Was there someone from that era who has completely dropped out of your life? What did you want to be when you grew up?

What happened after you finished school? What new person entered your life? In what ways were you startled or disappointed? Generally speaking, how have things turned out? Hop from scene to scene, working your way from the past to the present.

After you have completed this review (it shouldn't take more than fifteen to twenty minutes), quickly run through the scenes again—in order. Start with your parents, then move on through your birth, your preschool years, your school experiences, and your recent relationships and activities. What title would be appropriate for this story? What is the major theme? In your family, were you favored over other siblings? Were you an only child? Who was considered the black sheep of the family? Who was always getting into hot water? Who could talk their way out of anything? Were you or someone else in your family a hopeless romantic? A cockeyed optimist? A spoiled brat? An abuse victim? The one with potential? Should we consider your tale tragic or comic? A romantic romp, a sidesplitting farce, a morality play, or a meaningful documentary?

~

In Hollywood they don't usually start shooting until they have a complete script in hand. That's where life is different. Your story began at birth (whether you were ready or not), and it is likely that new plot twists have been popping up ever since. Even the title for your story may need to be adjusted as your life progresses. Nevertheless, your manager—now doubling as producer—can exert a steadying influence on the cast and crew by announcing the theme of the production. If, for instance, your manager envisions a life of love, compassion, well-being, and self-expression, those words can provide guidance to the script writers and casting director. Don't worry, there will still be plenty of room for improvisation. However, an overarching commitment can help keep the production on track, buoy spirits, and avert organizational chaos.

DISCOVERY 17: A Replay with the Manager in Charge

In a moment, we would like you to retake your seat in the *Twilight Zone* theater, but with an important difference. This time we want your manager, as producer, to take the reins. He or she can revise the drama to suit his or her purposes. Does your manager want to stick with the previous title, or should it be changed? What scenes does your manager want to revise or cut? Is he or she aiming for light comedy or Greek tragedy? The purpose of this rerun is to notice that the same set of events can be interpreted in various ways, leading to different reactions and outcomes. Falling off your bicycle, for example, is an opportunity to show bravery, a justification for avoiding physical risks, an opportunity to garner sympathy from parents, and so on.

Now, let's push the rewind button and replay the story one last time. This time, start with a wild plot premise. Use the very same incidents but see if you can weave an entirely different story. Perhaps this one can be about, let's say, maximizing carnal pleasure, defying authority, getting revenge, applying for sainthood, or having the last laugh. Review your life story—birth, school, career, and relationships—from one of these perspectives. Could you do it? Did you find ways to make the very same events fit an entirely new theme? Many succeed in this task because circumstances permit many interpretations. In that sense, our lives are not so much about what happens to us. They are about what we make of (and do with) what happens.

~

Let's imagine a young girl—Susie—growing up in an insensitive family. As a young child, she had buck teeth. Her poor vision forced her to wear thick, ugly glasses. On top of that, she was kind of pudgy. To make a long story short, Susie came to believe that she was an unattractive misfit. However, despite their general insensitivity, her family paid for Susie to have her vision repaired, and they sent her to an orthodontist for braces. As she got older, Susie grew lean and voluptuous, and was transformed from ugly duckling to knockout swan. All of a sudden, the messages Susie began getting from others, especially boys, were about how fabulous she looked, but she continued to live within her ugly duckling script. She certainly was polite to people when they said nice things about her looks, but whenever she looked in the mirror, she focused on her flaws and imperfections. Although she really was a knockout, her mental committee members still found ways to discount compliments and magnify rebuffs. Like most of us, Susie paid the most attention to statements that fit the self-perpetuating stereotypes derived from her childhood experiences.

If you asked her about her looks, she might think for a second or two and say something like, "Oh, I'm okay, I guess." But if she was being completely candid, she would have reported a litany of self-doubts—the legacy of her ugly duckling days.

Think for a moment about your own life script. Are you, like Susie, continuing to find validation for trademark traits and characteristics that are part of your history but may no longer be relevant? One of the authors knows an individual who grew up believing that he had no artistic or mechanical skills. His early attempts to build things were ridiculed by his older brothers. However, when he was in the army, he took an aptitude test that revealed superior scores in dexterity and spatial relations. Impressed by that feedback, he took up model making as a hobby. Over time, he became an expert craftsman. Ironically, when he went back to college and took some psychology courses, he discovered that the aptitude test he had taken while he was in the military was considered by psychologists to be invalid. In other words, the scores that inspired him to pursue woodworking were meaning-less. Of course, by the time he learned this, he was already a skilled artisan. Beliefs can work in both directions. That's why Henry Ford used to tell his associates, "Whether you believe you can do a thing or not, you are right."

DISCOVERY 18: Self-Beliefs

So, let's take a brief inventory of your self-beliefs, the basic threads out of which your self-narrative is woven. What do you consider to be your strengths? What skills and abilities seem to come naturally to you? What traits or characteristics seem beyond your reach? In what areas do you believe that you are a sham? What evidence do you use to support your current opinions about yourself?

Which of your self-beliefs would you be willing to take with a grain of salt? Remember, your most fervent beliefs are also apt to be the most limiting. Beliefs prevent surprises but diminish opportunities. The question is whether you are going to take charge or let your beliefs run your life. Our advice is to give beliefs their proper due, but as manager, feel free to operate underneath, around, and beyond those that seem to be getting in the way.

~

In the next two chapters we delve into aspects of reality and illusion. As Chuang Tzu, the second most famous

Taoist, said more than two thousand years ago: "Only after we awake do we know we have dreamed. Finally, there comes a great awakening, and then we know that life [itself] is a great dream."

CHAPTER 14

Reality and Illusion

Cut us open, and guess what? There are no thoughts or feelings inside. Nobody is fighting with anybody else. There are only body parts, chemicals, and processes—tubes and containers ferrying biochemical solutions back and forth. There are no emotions in the gut and no thoughts in the head. Self-esteem, willpower, and other figments of the human imagination are nowhere to be found.

We are faced with a peculiar situation. To us, our experiences seem absolutely real and solid, yet they have no concrete location in the body. For example, the color red cannot be found inside the blood vessels or even in the brain. Scientists and philosophers use the term *qualia* to describe our perceptions, which no matter how real they seem are neither inside the nervous system nor outside in the environment. Experiences of color (or anything else) are byproducts of how our biology interacts with the surrounding environment. If either our bodies or the world were structured differently, we would have different experiences. As the Spanish poet José Ortega Y Gasset wrote, "I am I plus my surroundings and if I do not preserve the latter, I do not preserve myself."

Most of us assume that red is a primary color and a fact of nature. However, most birds do not see red the way we do. Our visual system is set up in terms of three basic colors, whereas theirs uses four, and their color scheme is entirely different than ours. If birds could talk, there would be a furious debate with us about which basic colors, if any, are really "out there" in the world.

As this example shows, perceptions and experiences vary from one species to another. There is also a surprising amount of variation between one person and another and between one culture and another. Until recently, in the United States, eating raw fish was considered something best left to polar bears and seals. These days, however, sushi bars are the rage. The idea of eating insects is repulsive to many, but in Borneo, people snack contentedly on fried leafcutter ants.

A few years ago, an acclaimed exhibit of Paul Cézanne's paintings toured the United States. Art lovers were thrilled, but some museum visitors could not fathom what the fuss was about. In Europe, soccer matches so inflame passions that deadly riots sometimes break out. In the United States, similar contests often evoke yawns. A motion picture that some filmgoers will pay to see twenty or thirty times causes others to leave long before the credits roll.

Because of this kind of variability, it should be clear that our experiences say as much about us as they do about the world. The mother-in-law of one of the authors characteristically makes friends on every trip she takes. She befriends strangers on buses, trains, and planes.

She communicates her interest in them, and they generally return the favor. In this way, she turns chance meetings into memorable encounters. The rest of the family wouldn't dream of starting conversations with all those strangers. For them, train trips are rarely social occasions. The point is that life is like a giant projective test. You find what you seek. English novelist William Makepeace Thackeray put it this way: "The world is a looking glass and gives back to every man the reflection of his own face."

The Middle Way Revisited

This brings us back to the Buddhist middle way that we began describing way back in Chapter 5. On the one hand, life is real—when you fall down, it hurts, and when you find your lost keys, it feels good. On the other hand, personal beliefs are self-perpetuating illusions. Life is neither as solid as it looks nor as malleable as we would like. Buddhists describe this state of affairs as the *two truths*, which operate in tandem. It is the middle ground these two truths create that has, for the past 1800 years, empowered people and provided comfort to those in need.

For the Buddhist, the first truth highlights our ordinary reality—the world in which water is wet and rocks are hard. The second truth reflects the more mystical view that "everything is nothing" and outward appearances are deceptive. The middle way contends that everything in the universe is connected. Of course, the unity of the cosmos is disguised or obscured by our traditional distinctions—for instance, we separate plants and animals, yesterday and today, us and them, good and bad, important and unimportant, earth and sky. We talk as if day and night were separate events rather than just stages of the Earth's rotation observed from a particular location. As physicists know, matter and energy are flip sides of a single coin, and the separation of time and space is a convenient fiction.

Some twenty-five hundred years ago, Buddha began teaching that thinking of yourself as a separate individual is an illusion. He called this position *"anatman"* or "no-self." No-self was the core ingredient in the enlightenment of the person who came to be called Buddha. His name was Shakyamuni, and he was the spoiled son of a powerful king. By all accounts, he was an emotional mess. In today's terms, he would probably be considered chronically anxious or clinically depressed. Of course, at the time there were no psychotherapy clinics or psychotropic medications. Aching for emotional relief, he undertook a personal quest. By the way, he had no interest in founding a religion. It is merely that people were drawn to the novel answers his journey produced—new and surprising solutions to age-old puzzles.

Shakyamuni noticed that human beings are overly wed to their personal distinctions. People tend to think in terms of pigeonhole categories that do not match life's complexities. Therefore, Shakyamuni urged looking beyond narrow, individualistic concepts and concerns. He advocated adding the softer logic represented by "both/and" to the existing hard-edged categories of "either/or." Based on the first of the two truths—the Mode No. 1 logic we talked about in earlier chapters—people are individual egos chasing their our own dreams and battling their own demons. According to the second truth—

Mode No. 2 logic—we are all part of a universal process that is devoid of any real or final meaning and over which we have no true control.

In our daily lives, we certainly feel as if we are free-standing, freethinking organisms who make our own decisions and who—at least in theory—can choose to live any way we please. Our hardwiring and cultural background insures that we will experience ourselves this way. However, this sense of individualism is illusory. It is a bit like adolescents who, although they see themselves as making their own decisions, are just perpetuating the time-honored traditions of adolescent rebellion. Each adolescent thinks he or she has personally chosen to challenge authority. Yet, when you take a step back, it turns out that such actions are more or less predictable. Perhaps it is those youngsters who *don't* rebel who ought to be considered the mavericks! So, are adolescent expressions of independence acts of defiance or expressions of conformity? The middle way answer is "yes, definitely." In other words, both/and rather than either/or. Similarly, people can be thought of as both separate and connected. Just as cells are elements of a larger organism, individuals are the constituent parts of the human community.

To further our discussion of the middle way, examine the optical illusion on the next page. It is an example of an "illusory figure," and a good visual analogy for the middle way. Even after you notice that the white triangle is not "actually there," it refuses to go away. So, from the perspective of the middle way, the white triangle is *both* real and illusory. Similarly, in the middle way, life is both real and not real. Life works best when these twin

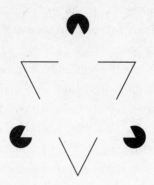

perspectives are allowed to soften each other by coexisting, side by side. The ordinary shades into the extraordinary, and vice versa. Life is both stable and flexible, there and not there, important and trivial. To quote Oscar Wilde, "Life is too important to be taken seriously."

A Real-Life Video Game

Scientists believe that one day we will be able to create artificial life forms that think and feel as we do. For the sake of argument, imagine that that day has already arrived. A videogame universe has been created that includes virtual human beings who experience their own lives the way we experience our own. These virtual humans live inside a video screen, just like the characters in today's arcade games. In their screened-in universe, they perceive an evolving universe of mountains and stars, thoughts and feelings, life and death—just as we do. Their experiences would be hardwired. As in the white triangle illusion, *their ordinary perception would not be wiped out even if they came to understand that it was all just a sophisticated simulation.*

Now imagine that the owner of one of these video games plugs in his or her newest game cartridge and then sits back to watch life inside the screen develop. The goal of this particular game is to see how quickly the simulated characters can discover, through the power of logic, that their ordinary experiences are illusory. In other words, how quickly can they achieve enlightenment—or, at least, simulated enlightenment? Of course, once they became enlightened, the characters in the game would probably be motivated to maximize love and well-being for everyone in their universe—a win/win for all concerned.

The question we raise is this: What is the true status of these game characters? Are their lives real or unreal? Once again, we assert that it is difficult to find a single answer to that question that is both accurate and complete. One can make a compelling case for each of two truths. From their own ordinary, local perspective they would certainly think of themselves as real. Furthermore, they would have plenty of evidence to back up that conclusion. After all, they feel pleasure and pain; they laugh and cry. They fervently believe they are making real choices and suffering real consequences.

On the other hand, from a position in front of the screen it would be apparent that their lives consisted of nothing more than the unfolding of a programmer's premise. If the plug were pulled, all their hard-won victories would disappear like the plot of a book that a reader closes and puts back on a shelf.

So, which is it—real or unreal? Why must we choose? Why not let it be both real and unreal? That is the position taken by noted scholar Daniel C. Dennett, who has devoted his career to grappling with problems of brain chemistry and human consciousness. He puts the dilemma this way: "Do we exist? Of course. . . . Are there entities, (selves) either in our brain or over and above our brains, that control our bodies, think our thoughts, make our decisions? Of course not! . . . When a simple question gets two answers, 'Obviously yes' and 'Obviously no,' a middle ground position is worth considering, even though it is bound to be initially counterintuitive" (1991, p. 413).

And that is the point, isn't it—that the truly radical and the sublimely self-evident can be joined? In fact, the ability to flip-flop between these two apparently opposite perspectives yields an especially powerful and flexible weapon for combating everyday attachments.

It is said that even the Buddha, being human, felt and suffered. However, because of his great mastery, he was able to let go of upsets in a split second. The trick is becoming accustomed to rapid shifts between Mode No. 1 and Mode No. 2 logic. As Dennett argues, when you look inside the human brain, there is nobody home. The more deeply you inquire into the human condition, the clearer it becomes that there is only *anatman*—no-self. Yet, at the same time, *someone* is obviously reading these pages and working hard to come to grips with this material.

Unlike chemical substances, the Buddhist middle way philosophy is a natural mood-mitigant with no harmful side effects. It defies ordinary logic but can be grasped intuitively. It is a valuable tool for lightening up. It helps human beings maximize love and well-being for themselves and others. It leavens passion with tranquility. In the next chapter, we talk more about how to make this perspective work for you.

CHAPTER 15

Plenty of Nothing

Of everything we have discussed, the most difficult point to grasp is that *nothing inherently or independently exists.* John Wheeler, the renowned physicist who coined the term *black hole,* says simply, "There is no *out there* out there." Buddhists use the word *shunyata* to refer to this ultimate emptiness, which is coupled with the fundamentally illusory nature of the world. The paradox of being and nonbeing has, over the centuries, confounded scientists, philosophers, religious leaders, and ordinary citizens. However, by encouraging us to juggle multiple perspectives, the middle way permits us to have our cake and eat it, too. We can be skeptical about the existence of an ultimate reality, but at the same time avoid the scary nihilism of facing a life without significance. The middle way assures safe passage by helping us steer between the Scylla of cynicism and the Charybdis of excessive (and often painful) attachment. Only a middle way can leaven the ferocious grip of Mode No. 1 logic by coupling it with liberating Mode No. 2 possibilities.

The next several chapters are aimed at helping you use

the middle way in your own life. Many people assume that enlightenment is supposed to feel like being struck by a lightning bolt. It is said to require long periods of arduous and mysterious meditation practices. Once enlightenment hits, it is supposed to put you in a state of permanent bliss. But enlightenment is not anything like that. It is about becoming increasingly skillful at juggling paradoxical viewpoints. An enlightened individual realizes that no single feeling or insight can be expected to persist. For both enlightened and unenlightened individuals, there is a constant flow of experiences, thoughts, and feelings. In fact, enlightenment is such a broad outlook that it even has room for periods of non-enlightenment. However, even when enlightened individuals aren't feeling particularly enlightened, they trust that their commitment to absolute and unconditional love and compassion is intact, and that, sooner or later, they will regain their footing. They also know that the best way to perpetuate misery is to frantically try to get rid of it. Again, the operative principle is that whatever you resist persists and whatever you let be lets you be. So, they relax (or they don't) and wait for enlightenment to pay a return visit.

Enlightenment includes all of life's experiences. It includes having a fit because a package arrives damaged. It includes the frustration of being awakened at three in the morning by some idiot who dialed a wrong number. It includes the agony of losing your wallet or purse. Enlightenment does not guarantee a state of perpetual ecstasy, which is probably what you were attempting with chemical substances.

Enlightenment also entails keeping your word, no matter what you happen to be feeling or experiencing at the moment. In fact, if you did little else but keep your commitment to maximize love and well-being for self and others, it would be hard to avoid experiencing enlightenment. Honoring a loving agreement vividly puts you in touch with your place in the universe.

We advise being judicious in making commitments but being scrupulous about keeping those you have made. Renegotiate any contracts with yourself or others that have become stale or outdated. A proper renegotiation requires that all involved parties be satisfied with the new arrangements. Similarly, if and when you break your word, make amends as soon as possible, cleaning up any resulting mess. Insure that everyone affected has received his or her proper due. Although there are no hard and fast rules for how best to repair the damage caused by a given transgression, everyone involved typically feels complete when the proposed remedies truly fit the occasion.

One of the authors had to keep a client waiting while he handled a crisis at the clinic. The client had traveled a considerable distance to meet with the author. However, by the time the crisis was resolved, the time for his session had evaporated. The author asked the client if he would be able and willing to return at lunchtime the following day. That would give them plenty of time to meet. In addition, because of the inconvenience the client experienced, the rescheduled session would be free of charge and, since it would be noontime, a free lunch would be provided. The client was more than willing to agree to this new arrangement. Even though the cancellation of the client's first session wasn't anyone's fault and wasn't done capriciously, it still represented the abrogation of a contract. The renegotiation—in this case, between client and therapist—had to take into account any damages the parties suffered. Whenever possible, everyone should end up feeling that they are better off than when they started. When a contract has been successfully renegotiated, the incident seems complete. There are no loose ends or hurt feelings.

Sometimes it is sufficient that broken contracts simply be acknowledged. "I know I said I would be here at seven P.M. and I wasn't." At other times, more concrete repair work is needed. It isn't that breaking your word is a crime that requires punishment. However, only by honoring your pledges can you become a powerful player in your own life and in the lives of others.

A challenge of the middle way is staying in touch with your essential connectedness. We are programmed by eons of evolution to focus on our own petty concerns and not see the relatedness that defines us. This is the point of view emphasized by Thich Nhat Hanh, perhaps the most famous and most beloved Zen master in the world today. His engaged Buddhism emphasizes social responsibility. Master Thay, as he is known by his admirers, writes the following:

> When we go to a meditation center, we may have the impression that we leave everything behind— family, society, and all the complications involved in them—and come as an individual in order to practice and to search for peace. This is already an illusion, because in Buddhism there is no such thing as an individual.

Master Thay points out that something as simple as a piece of paper contains and reflects all the elements of the universe, including the sun, the soil, and the water that enables trees to grow and nourishes the loggers who eventually harvest them. Even a blank or "empty" piece of paper, he argues, is "full of everything, the entire cosmos." Furthermore, because nothing can stand alone, no "thing" can be said to be truly solid. Everything is made up of multiple elements that are not, by themselves, "it." At the same time, every object is absolutely essential to the cosmic web of interrelationships.

DISCOVERY 19: One Is the Loneliest Number

If we can prove to you that nothing stands alone, we can also prove the value and legitimacy of what we have been calling Mode No. 2 logic. Taking our cue from Master Thay, we ask that you consider a sheet of paper. Can it stand by itself in the universe? Can it exist "from its own side," as the Buddhists would say? Does it have solid existence, apart from anything and everything else, including the empty space that surrounds it? Obviously not. To be paper, it has to have boundaries—it has to be distinguishable from everything around it that isn't paper. If there was nothing else with which it could be compared, it would lose its identity. Without distinct boundaries, it would simply ooze into the surrounding neighborhood and disappear like a drop of ink in a glass of water.

Take anything, perhaps this book, and try to visualize it without its boundaries. The boundaries of an item are the edges or surfaces that both separate it and, at the same time, connect it to everything else. We hope you can see that, without such boundaries, any item surrenders its uniqueness and evaporates. Our point is that anything, no matter how solidly sensed, depends—for its very definition—on being in relationship with everything else. That is why it is hard to achieve peace of mind while stubbornly insisting that you "don't need anyone." That is also why compassion for self implies compassion for all. Thomas Paine put it well when he said that "the world is my country, all mankind are my brethren, and to do good is my religion."

~

The whole idea of a middle way is to help you lighten up. In fact, it is the harsh way in which life is ordinarily experienced that pushes many of us off the sobriety wagon. However, even the pain of life's tribulations can be harnessed to a good cause. After all, most people are unwilling to go the distance unless motivated by a certain amount of suffering. As with any quest, those who are too content usually stay home. Recall that Buddha's journey hinged on the angst of one man. Also, it is probably your own distress patterns that have prompted you to stick with this sometimes-vexing author-reader dialogue.

So here is the winning formula:

- First, use your suffering to propel you to reach beyond the ordinary.

- Second, stay in touch with the larger picture revealed by Buddhism's twin truths.
- Third, practice applying a both/and perspective to even small, everyday facts and events.
- Fourth, find ways to share any resulting insights with others (without making a complete nuisance of yourself).
- Fifth, take all lists of recommendations, including this one, with a grain of salt.

Bringing It Home

The middle way implies motion and movement. After all, it is a path—not a point or spot. The middle way teaches that we live in a world of flux, not static realities. In a world of motion, standing still produces vertigo. The alternative is oscillation—an artful bouncing back and forth between perspectives. At breakfast, lament the fact that the toast is burnt. At the same time, peer through the portal of the larger reality long enough to notice that burnt toast is the least of your problems. Having done that, try tasting the burnt toast (interesting) or simply slip another piece of bread into the toaster and get on with it.

Grouse about glitches and frustrations just for the hell of it. Fight injustice (but don't expect to win anytime soon). Weep in connection with searing losses—the full expression of grief is a fundamental (and underrated) way to validate one's aliveness. Float between the conventional perspective, a world of frenetic victories and personalized defeats, and the extraordinary perspective, where it is understood that both wins and losses are needed to keep the game going.

Some of the people we see in our practices have been severely punished by life. They have been exposed to incest, physical and emotional abuse, grinding poverty, and so on. Naturally, we have great empathy for the suffering such individuals have endured. However, sympathy from others is not enough. They need to see that even after having lived through terrible trials, they can still take a stand for unconditional love and compassion. They can harness the power of their travails. Alexis de Tocqueville once said that although "we succeed in enterprises which demand the positive qualities we possess . . . we excel in those which can also make use of our defects."

Nelson Mandela is a good example of what is possible for human beings to achieve. After spending twenty-seven years in prison for crimes he did not commit and seeing millions of his people murdered, brutalized, and disenfranchised by a racist regime, he was able to let go of any desire for revenge in order to help create a government of reconciliation in South Africa. He sets an inspirational example for those of us whose days can be ruined by a traffic ticket or a missed phone call. Of course, Mandela operates on the international stage. Yet each of us has daily opportunities to demonstrate the value of our commitments. To quote Mary Shelley, the nineteenth-century British writer, "Nothing contributes so much to tranquilizing the mind as a steady purpose—a point on which the soul may fix its intellectual eye."

In the next and penultimate chapter we return to the basic theme of acceptance—choosing to have things be the way they are so that they can evolve into something even more interesting and fulfilling.

CHAPTER 16

Acceptance: Choosing Life

The Senoi tribe lives in the Malaysian jungle. Anthropologists have reported that they use dreams as a vehicle for teaching children how to cope with life (Garfield, 1995). If, for example, a Senoi child describes a dream in which he was chased by a tiger, his father would ask what he did when the tiger appeared. Let's assume that the boy tells his father that he ran away. The father might then say something like the following: "It was good you had that dream, son, but you made a big mistake. . . . the tigers you see in your dreams at night can only hurt you if you run from them. They will continue to chase you only so long as you are afraid of them. The next time you have this dream . . . you must turn around and face the tiger" (p. 108).

The Senoi believe in facing and accepting, not denying or avoiding. Suppose the boy argues that the tiger was too big for him to handle. The father would explain that he can call upon his "dream friends" (p. 108) to help. However, until they arrive, the rule is to stay and do the best you can. Mastery consists of acknowledging adversity rather than fleeing from it. In the Senoi philosophy, a foe that is vanquished becomes your friend. Its spirit joins yours, and you are entitled to ask it to grant you a gift—perhaps a poem, a beautiful thought, a melody, a helpful image, or a piece of advice. The gift enriches your life and can later be shared with other members of the community.

According to Garfield, "Dream images are enemies only so long as you fear them" (p. 111). Adversities, when confronted, diminish in size. "Turning to face the tiger, the angry witch, and other such figures [transforms] them into a kitten, a mother, and other smaller, less alarming images." Garfield reports that dreamers who face and accept dream dangers "feel enhanced confidence in their waking lives" (p. 141).

Note the parallels between Garfield's description of the Senoi view and the metaphor of the playground bully we used earlier in this book. In both cases, the take-home message is that accepting and facing difficult circumstances shrinks problems to manageable proportions. It helps turn predicaments into opportunities.

Defining Acceptance

The dictionary defines acceptance as receiving something (especially with gladness) or regarding something as proper, usual, right, or true. Sometimes, acceptance implies putting up with events—enduring adversity with patience and forbearance. For instance, the phrase "accepting one's fate" carries that connotation. However, we are talking here about active acceptance, not passive resignation. *The objective is to boldly and courageously affirm and choose life unconditionally, to accept it as perfect however it happens to show up.* In practice, the term acceptance means temporarily suspending judgments of right and wrong. It implies a kind of flat, nonevaluative willingness to just let things be, regardless of whether or not they seem fair, desirable, or convenient. It means using the perspective of Mode No. 2 to mitigate the hardwired, negative responses we all have to events and circumstances we consider undesirable or disadvantageous.

Full acceptance—choosing life in its entirety—is the key to serenity. It is also the essence of the middle way as it relates to your everyday existence. When we talk about choosing life, we mean choosing everything that exists and everything that can be *thought about,* including inanimate objects and abstractions. Death is included. So is the concept of God, even if you do not happen to be a believer. Our definition has room for goblins, Rip Van Winkle, Sherlock Holmes, and any other fictional characters you might conceivably think about. Even thoughts such as "I can't possibly accept that" are included.

Perhaps all this seems obvious. However, let's linger over an important implication of the definitions we are proposing. If your life includes everything that you know about or think about, and you agree to accept life unconditionally, then you are agreeing to accept everything that you perceive to be happening, from the very best to the very worst. Actually, the enlightened person recognizes that both good and bad are necessary threads in life's fabric. Your acceptance is a statement of uncompromising inclusion.

Inclusion and Exclusion

Of course, when most people think about acceptance, they are not usually thinking about a philosophy of radical inclusiveness and affirmation. Instead, they envision forming some kind of elite club and deciding who deserves membership privileges. They would certainly not admit the jerk from across the street who insists on taking up two parking spots. The club would not include, let's say, welfare bums, corrupt politicians, greedy relatives, corporate polluters, religious nuts, tax auditors, and so on. People with troublesome diseases such as pancreatic cancer and multiple sclerosis would not be welcome. In short, acceptance is generally limited to the pleasant, the expected, and the manageable.

The trouble is that exclusionary tactics carry high costs. The middle way philosophy asserts that anything you exclude weakens you, leaving you ill-equipped to deal with life's eventualities and making it more difficult to honor your commitments. Avoiding any one aspect of life distorts your understanding and appreciation of the rest of it.

To see how costly avoidance can be, consider how society reacted to the medical establishment's attempts to treat and control venereal disease, particularly syphilis. For years, people's approach to this affliction consisted mainly of studied avoidance. They were uncomfortable uttering the word in polite society. It was as if talking about it was almost as distressing as having it. Their hesitance to share information about syphilis slowed scientists' search for effective treatments. Even later, when antibiotics became widely available, many people suffering from syphilis failed to get the treatment they needed because they were too embarrassed to go to their doctors. Worse yet, they continued to infect others. Recently, similar cycles of shame, blame, and avoidance have hampered attempts to control the AIDS epidemic.

Nonacceptance has also proven to be an obstacle in dealing with child and sexual abuse. In many communities, people continue to behave as if abusive situations are rare, mysterious, aberrant acts perpetrated by a small number of subhuman individuals. This approach fosters secrecy, hinders true insight, and delays effective action. It would be better if we accepted that abuse is part of life—a homegrown affliction, not the curse of the devil or evidence of an alien invasion. In fact, the history of abuse parallels the history of the species. In what epoch have we not had slavery, torture, genocide, infanticide, religious persecution, and every other conceivable form of inhumanity? According to Mode No. 2 thinking, the Inquisition and the Holocaust were never about "them." These atrocities were—and are—about us and life. Within all of us are the seeds of evil and deceit as well as the seeds of love and compassion. As they used to say in acting class, anyone who has ever swatted a fly understands murder.

The Acceptance of Suffering

As we have indicated, the First Noble Truth in Buddhism is that suffering is an inevitable aspect of being human. You can observe the truth of this by reviewing almost any segment of your own life or, if you prefer, the history of the human race. Presumably our troubles began when we acquired the gift (or curse) of self-awareness. As English essayist William Hazlitt reminds us, "Man is the only animal that laughs and weeps; for he is the only animal that is struck with the difference between what things are and what they ought to be."

The biblical account of creation attributes our self-awareness and egocentrism to Eve's fateful sampling of the forbidden fruit. That apple bite forever alienated human beings from the natural order. Ever since then, we have trekked through life as individual egos, convinced that we could eliminate pain, banish disease, cheat death, and destroy our enemies. The motto is, "Avoid showing weakness or admitting defeat." From this perspective, life is a constant fight for survival and supremacy. Unfortunately, life is the one game that you cannot win through that kind of brute force. Life is one of those games where winning hinges on your willingness to surrender. As we have said, whatever you resist persists.

Only unconditional acceptance, in which the inevitability of pain, evil, and suffering are fully acknowledged, can produce contentment. We advocate a radical acceptance that recognizes pain and loss as integral components of life. In other words, some days you eat the bear and some days the bear eats you.

So, how do you achieve this radical acceptance? Keeping in mind your commitment to maximize love and well-being, simply have your manager declare a willingness to allow life to show up in all its myriad forms, including ugliness, evil, injustice, and misfortune. Welcome troubles and challenges as part of the game. Surely, even in your least enlightened moments, you have realized that a life of constant wins would be a devastatingly boring affair.

In true acceptance, you become interested in every event that shows up. Your attitude is not "How could this possibly happen to me?" It is more like "Yep, here we go again and I wouldn't have it any other way." By definition, the truly acceptant are never in the role of victim—even when adversity strikes. They choose life, adversity and all! Under every conceivable condition, they continue to keep the faith, recognizing that whatever happens is part of the bargain. Of course, from time to time, they are completely overwhelmed. They become attached to their circumstances. They curse and scream. They consider themselves and everyone else wrong. Their curiosity about life disappears in a storm of fury or grief. However, their derailment is only temporary, and soon they are back on track. Their manager is back on duty and has reminded them of their essential connectedness and their longstanding commitment to the expression of love and compassion.

Although a life of integrity and acceptance reduces the frequency, intensity, and duration of upsets, it does not eliminate them. To take a drastic example, consider what would happen if your spouse died, a very heavy blow for virtually anyone to bear. By all means, you should grieve and carry on about it. Celebrate the relationship you had (and continue to have) with your loved one. Find ways to memorialize your spouse's passing. Meld his or her goals into your own so that the next phase of your life validates and expands upon the meanings you and your spouse created together. By no means use the loss to justify abandoning your agreements. Do not permit rage and self-pity to dethrone your manager. In fact, use anger and other negative emotions to fuel your efforts to reach the goals you and your spouse prioritized.

DISCOVERY 20: Expanding Acceptance

In *Through the Looking Glass,* the White Queen explains that when she was Alice's age she practiced believing impossible things for at least half an hour each day. Sometimes, she boasted, she managed to believe "as many as six impossible things before breakfast" (Carroll, 1871/1994, p. 250). In this exercise, we are not asking that you believe the impossible. However, we want you to practice something almost as difficult—accepting and affirming the full range of life's possibilities. Of course, as you do this exercise, you should pay close attention to the items you would ordinarily be tempted to exclude, deny, or resist. Choosing life in its entirety means giving up your "yes, buts," and exchanging them for simple but extraordinary "yeses."

In a sense, this entire workbook has been preparation for the mastery of acceptance. Full acceptance means dropping any victim act. After all, if you assume that life is the way it is supposed to be—always—then what is there to complain about? Of course, when you are operating in Mode No. 1, feel free to do some recreational grousing. Everyone understands the fun of bitching and moaning, now and again. However, use your Mode No. 2 perspective to prevent you from taking any "poor me" routine seriously. Serenity and empowerment require giving up the presumption that you have the right to dictate how your life should unfold.

With that prelude in mind, it is time for your manager to answer each of the following questions. Take a deep breath, because the list is lengthy and challenging.

- Do you accept that ordinary people are often cruel, inconsiderate, and heartless?
- Do you accept that children all over the world are dying of malnutrition?
- Do you accept that the notion of God may be a fable?
- Do you accept that ordinary people are frequently devious and self-serving?
- Do you accept that it is your right and obligation to help improve the world (even if you do not have the foggiest notion about how to do it)?
- Do you accept that you could lose your job or your financial security at any time?
- Do you accept that someone you trust will betray you?
- Do you accept the seeming inevitability of wars and bloodshed?
- Do you accept that people are sometimes genuinely altruistic?
- Do you accept that people are evil?
- Do you accept your own evil motives?
- Do you accept the possibility of time travel?
- Do you accept the fact that innocent children are abused daily?

- Do you accept that people are spreading false rumors about you?
- Do you accept dying?
- Do you *really* accept dying?
- Do you accept that you may develop or contract a life-threatening illness?
- Do you accept that millions of people are better off than you are?
- Do you accept that you have made some really serious mistakes?
- Do you accept that you will continue making serious mistakes?
- Do you accept generosity from others?
- Do you truly accept the forgiveness of others?
- Do you accept having injured others?
- Do you accept having intentionally injured others?
- Do you accept that you will eventually lose everything?
- Do you accept the possibility of sudden and serious injury?
- Do you accept that friends and confidants will lie to you?
- Do you accept that your choices will be criticized?
- Do you accept that some people will want to give you valuable gifts?
- Do you accept being considered worthy by people you admire or respect?
- Can you accept being or becoming a parent?
- Do you accept that you are still an adolescent (despite your chronological age)?

- Do you accept that you are highly susceptible to being conned?
- Do you accept that people are violent?
- Do you accept that you have purposely avoided telling others what they need to hear?
- Do you accept your basic goodness?
- Do you accept being whole, sufficient, and complete?
- Do you accept not having lived up to your potential?
- Do you accept homicide and suicide as part of the human condition?
- Do you accept the fact that newborns are regularly abandoned or killed?
- Do you accept that people make fun of you behind your back?
- Do you accept that people do not take you seriously?
- Do you accept the possibility of being in a fire or drowning?
- Do you accept the possibility of being in a serious auto accident?
- Do you accept that someone close to you may stop speaking to you?
- Do you accept that your life is finite and futile?
- Do you accept that some of your best efforts have been totally in vain?
- Do you accept the fact that innocent people are tortured in many countries around the world?
- Do you accept sexual inadequacy?
- Do you accept that many criminals prosper?

- Do you accept being a role model for others?
- Do you accept being the source of love and compassion?

What else that we have neglected to list do you need to work at accepting? Finally, are you willing to accept the currently incomplete state of your acceptance?

~

Avoiding a Steady State

Even if we were able to accept everything—unconditionally, and at all times—our hard-won sense of acceptance would quickly evaporate. This is because one cannot consciously focus on a steady state. It is like what people who live by the railroad tracks report: They no longer hear the trains. They only "hear" breaks in the pattern—for instance, when a train fails to arrive on time.

So, even radical acceptance requires fluctuation or oscillation. Remember, Mode No. 1 and Mode No. 2 perceptions are mutually interdependent. Let yourself shift back and forth between ordinary, small-minded fault finding and the glorious perception that we are interconnected beings pursuing life's grand adventure while maximizing compassion. Treat radical acceptance like a refreshing breeze that wafts through a room from time to time, reinvigorating body and soul. It is deeply paradoxical that the magnificence of the whole can only be appreciated in small doses.

Note that full acceptance does not preclude fighting back when a bully throws sand in your face—acceptance involves more than sitting around and worshiping the status quo. Your Mode No. 1 responsibilities include defending yourself and competing vigorously with others whenever it is appropriate. At the same time, your Mode No. 2 consciousness is a reminder that even adversaries are an essential component of the world you pledged to embrace.

There is a Zen tale of a great samurai warrior whose family was killed by a bandit. For years, he hunted the killer, finally finding him in an alley in a far-off city. The samurai unsheathed his sword and was about to strike when he suddenly turned and walked away. The bandit cried out: "Why, after pursuing me for all these years, are you not avenging your family's death?" The samurai turned and stated, simply, "I have lost my temper." It has been said that if there is a true evil in the world, it is self-righteousness.

We recall a drug-addicted client who lost custody of his two young children. Initially, he complained bitterly about the judge's decision: "Why is she taking my kids away? They are my life." In fact, the judge fully understood his feelings, but could also see that his children were not being adequately parented. She acknowledged the father's love but didn't hesitate to remove the children from his care. Eventually, the father realized that the judge was not his enemy. In fact, her no-nonsense decision was the wake-up call he needed to see that the best thing he could do for his children was to sober up and get his act together. Please note that taking a firm stand is not incompatible with compassion.

As we have said from the outset, the objective is to participate—play hard, enjoy the game, and accept the inevitability of wins and losses. When a game ends, go to the locker room and get ready for the next adventure. Follow a middle way, and balance the heavy with the light. Be willing for life to be a joyful combination of "What's next?" and "So what?"

CHAPTER 17

Retracing the Journey

Congratulations! You have come to the end of what we hope has been an extraordinary journey of self-discovery. We wrote this primer to assist you in escaping the dragons of addiction. It would give us great pleasure to know that you have tucked it into your backpack as you set off on your personal enlightenment expedition.

A primary tool of the voyage is an Eastern philosophy called the middle way. In contrast to the either/or logic of the West, which prohibits allowing contradictory propositions to coexist, the middle way encourages such co-existence. For example, it preaches the virtue of thinking of yourself as both utterly individualistic and thoroughly relational. The middle way adds the softer logic of both/and to the hard-edged categories of either/or. It invites seesawing between opposing alternatives rather than insisting that one be abandoned in favor of the other. Niels Bohr, the renowned physicist who founded quantum theory, put it this way: "There are trivial truths and great truths. The opposite of a trivial truth is plainly false. The opposite of a great truth is also true."

Physicists were among the first groups of Westerners to rebel against the strictures of traditional logic. They were stumped to discover that, in their experiments, light sometimes acted like a wave and sometimes like a particle (see, for example, Capra, 1975). They could not answer the question, "Which is it, really?" In a move Eastern philosophers would applaud, they finally decided to call it a "wavicle." In other words, both/and.

In higher physics and ordinary life, there are many logical contradictions and paradoxes that demand a flexibility of language and perception that strains the categories of Western, linear thought. It is at times like these that the middle way is particularly helpful.

The middle way thrives on paradox, absurdity, and contradiction. It gives equal attention to wholes and parts. Although it provides a deep, reassuring perspective, it is not a hopelessly complex or abstract philosophy. Most people can readily grasp its few basic principles, and it isn't difficult to apply to the conundrums of everyday life. Approaching life from the standpoint of the middle way can lighten problems and drain tensions. As stress decreases, so does the urge to self-medicate.

Self-awareness is arguably mankind's greatest gift, but also its worst liability. We have been doomed to troop through life as individual egos, constantly worrying about how well or how poorly we are doing. However, because Eastern philosophies like the middle way remind us of our essential connectedness, they have the power to ease the pain of our estrangement.

In presenting the philosophy of the middle way, we suggested that you take a stand for love, compassion, and well-being. In a sense, you have no choice about it. Love is simply a manifestation of your essential connectedness. Because you are already connected (or how would you have gotten here?), the only choice you have is whether or not to acknowledge and express your connectedness.

From this perspective, you are and have always been whole, complete, and sufficient. This is true whether or not you believe it, like it, or understand it. Nevertheless, you have the option of operating as if you were defective or deficient. Many people do just that. They assume that they are not entitled to be satisfied unless they win more awards, improve themselves, get a promotion, find a partner, and so on. Obviously, we recommend against continuing to consider yourself to be damaged goods. It is more fun to play the game of life from sufficiency rather than deficiency—and the price of admission is the same.

We also asked that you make a practice of keeping your word, no matter what. Honor the stand you have taken, even though it is often easier to give up, make excuses, blame others, berate yourself, or adopt the victim role. We should also add that keeping your agreements includes holding others accountable for the pledges they make. It is a disservice to simply look the other way when people betray their own commitments. We are, in fact, our brothers' (and sisters') keepers.

In the early chapters of this book, we suggested that you consider reinventing yourself as a person whose survival does not hinge on consuming drugs or alcohol. People usually rely on chemical substances when they feel a need to avoid life's heaviness. Therefore, we have described other approaches to lightening up. In the service of this goal, we asked that you consider the possibility that you are fundamentally innocent in the matter of your addiction. We tried to show how and why your mind—a core aspect of your humanity—becomes so belligerent and accusatory.

Your mind is like an unruly executive committee or board of trustees. Some members of the board, in their well-intentioned efforts to protect you from harm, go overboard. They see danger everywhere and bombard you with an unending series of complaints, reservations, criticisms, and condemnations. They rarely recognize that their efforts often backfire, draining you of energy, creating morale problems, and making drugs and alcohol seem more attractive.

To combat these nay-saying mind banditos, we suggested appointing a leader, an internal manager who could bring some semblance of order to the warring factions of your executive committee. By taking a stand for maximizing love and well-being (for yourself and others), the manager gains the moral authority to negotiate compromises between conflicting internal voices. The manager helps forestall panic and overreaction by keeping the larger picture in focus.

We provided some tools to enhance the manager's clout. These included the practice of mindfulness, detached observation, and reflection. Armed with that equipment, we were then able to return to the issue of basic guilt and innocence. This time, however, we were interested in your considering a more sweeping declaration— your unconditional innocence in all things. Of course, we knew you would wonder about the related issues of responsibility and accountability. Therefore, we tried to show that from a middle way perspective, it is possible to declare innocence and, at the same time, keep agreements and act responsibly.

The idea of no-self, or *anatman*, is a key concept of Eastern enlightenment. It leaves you blessedly free, but also empty of any inherent significance. Surmounting the paradox involves juggling contradictory alternatives. In Taoism, it is the dynamic, ongoing tension created by the interplay of opposites that creates the pulse of life. The analogy many find helpful is bicycle riding or tightrope walking. The trick is to be constantly balancing, adjusting and readjusting from side to side as you swing down the middle path toward ever increasing love and well-being.

To help rejuvenate your passion for living, we next hammered away at the harm that guilt, shame, and hope-lessness can do. These are the most pernicious internal voices, but also the most convincing. We asked your manager to catalog your personal "sins," getting them on the table, once and for all, so that you would be prepared to confront any future propaganda put out by your mind demons.

Gaining mastery involves having at least a rudimentary understanding of how emotions work. Although it is nat-ural (and necessary) to have emotions, there is no need for them to have you! When people understand more about their bodily machinery, they come to realize that the conflicts they experience are not actually fights be-tween their thoughts and emotions, even though we sometimes talk about them that way. In fact, your body, including the nervous system, can be counted on to do a pretty good job of supporting your intentions. It is almost always safe and appropriate to allow your emotions—

changes in bodily calibrations—to be felt. More detrimental is the attempt to suppress reactions and to deny experience. The rule, of course, is that whatever you resist persists and whatever you let be lets you be. At the same time, being able to observe your reactivity—through the practice of detachment—provides a very powerful double perspective.

It is not surprising that people can become obsessed with daytime soap operas, even though they realize that the plots are implausible and have been specifically written to manipulate our attention. The truth is that we are drawn in to these stories because our own lives are soap operas. By recognizing the storied nature of our existence, we gain an additional degree of detachment. With sufficient perspective, we can try out a different characterization or revise the script we have been using. Why should Act III parallel Acts I and II, especially if you were less than thrilled with how those narratives unfolded?

The middle way invites scrutiny about our basic assumptions. Aldous Huxley noted that "most human beings have an almost infinite capacity for taking things for granted." Yet, nothing is more eye-opening (and humbling) than the realization that we never see things the way they really are. That is the insight we worked to establish in our chapter on reality and illusion. Buddhists talk about this in terms of there being two truths—what we labeled Mode No. 1 and Mode No. 2. Each mode is incomplete without the other. Each tells only half the story. By balancing them, you keep yourself centered on a middle path.

Mode No. 1 is about our conventional, everyday reality—a world of separate things and events. Mode No. 2 denies the existence of that very reality. It speaks to the interrelationships that define who we are. John Donne was, of course, correct to write that "no man is an island." However, it is also useful to notice that even an island can have no independent identity. The Buddhists use the term *shunyata* to remind us that nothing can exist "from its own side." Everything perceived is perceived through relationship.

We should note that some of the finest minds of our century have found it difficult to integrate the meaning of Mode Nos. 1 and 2. Nobel Prize–winning biologist Michael Gazzaniga writes, "I don't want to live in a society that doesn't think it exists." This is where the middle way comes to the rescue. It lets you have your cake and eat it, too.

In the previous chapter, we emphasized the challenge of acceptance. Our species originated in the tooth-and-claw environment of our tribal ancestors. In those days, survival was the name of the game. Life was constantly about "us" versus "them." Given this evolutionary history, it is difficult for any of us to embrace a thoroughly inclusive worldview. Yet, unconditional acceptance—choosing life the way it is, from the best to the worst—holds the key to contentment and tranquility. Whatever is denied, avoided, or excluded tends to become more dominant and controlling. As we keep saying, whatever you resist persists. Paradoxically, it is easier to live joyfully once you have acknowledged the inevitability of pain, evil, and suffering. Follow the middle way, shifting back and forth between Mode No. 1 and Mode No. 2, between protecting your survival and participating more openly in the glorious show taking place all around you. Let these two contrasting perspectives play off each other.

What we offer is not an easy path. But to find diamonds sharp enough to cut the bonds that keep you stuck in addictive patterns, it takes more than a quick walk in the park. Nevertheless, we assert that the happy ending you have dreamed about is actually within your grasp. We have attempted to re-ignite your desire to get there and propose using the middle way to illuminate the path. In the meantime, keep your word and remain open to experience and opportunity. Let these mind-altering ideas replace mind-altering substances.

The Tao of Sobriety in a Nutshell: A Handy Crib Sheet

1. Alcohol and drugs mitigate your experience of reality. If you have become dependent on alcohol and drugs, you are running from problematic aspects of your own experience.

2. Your mind is a space where many competing internal conversations vie for power.

3. You can elect a mental manager who takes a stand for maximizing love and well-being for yourself and others.

4. Your manager is up against some ferocious mind demons who preach negative messages of guilt, shame, and hopelessness.

5. To tame this unruly bunch of naysayers, your manager needs to learn mindfulness—the practice of detached observation.

6. By utilizing detachment, you can have upsets without becoming enslaved by them.

7. You are not literally guilty of anything.

8. Becoming the master of your own experience involves noticing that your life is a drama that you have helped create.

9. Life can be seen as a paradoxical both/and affair. You can play hard and, at the same time, recognize that life is only a game. You can create meaning and, at the same time, recognize that ultimately all meanings are temporary and irrelevant. You can respect your everyday experience and, at the same time, see beyond your limited horizon.

10. Enlightenment is about your willingness to keep your word and to choose life in its entirety—the good with the bad.

11. Enlightenment involves compassionate action—doing your part to make the world work for all its inhabitants.

References

Capra, Fritjof, *The Tao of Physics*. New York: Bantam Books (1975).

Carroll, Lewis, *Through the Looking Glass*. New York: Quality Paperback Book Club (1871/1994).

Carse, James P., *Finite and Infinite Games: A Vision of Life as Play and Possibility*. New York: Ballantine Books (1986).

Dennett, Daniel C., *Consciousness Explained*, Boston: Back Bay Books (Little Brown & Company) (1991).

Garfield, Patricia L., *Creative Dreaming*. New York: Simon & Schuster (1995).

Kelly, George A., *Clinical Psychology and Personality: The Selected Papers of George Kelly* (Brendan Maher, Ed.). New York: John Wiley & Sons (1969).

Marlatt, Alan, and Judith Gordon (Eds.), *Relapse Prevention: Maintenance Strategies in the Treatment of Addictive Behaviors*. New York: Guilford (1985).

Ram Dass, *Be Here Now*. New York: Crown (1971).

References

Smothermon, Ron, *Winning Through Enlightenment*. San Francisco: Context Publications (1979).

Weekes, Claire, *Simple, Effective Treatment of Agoraphobia*. New York: Bantam Books (1976).